KOSTES PALAMAS

LIFE IMMOVABLE

FIRST PART

Copyright © 2013 Read Books Ltd.
This book is copyright and may not be
reproduced or copied in any way without
the express permission of the publisher in writing

British Library Cataloguing-in-Publication Data
A catalogue record for this book is available from the
British Library

TO MRS. EVELETH WINSLOW

THIS VOLUME OF TRANSLATIONS IS
DEDICATED
AS A TOKEN OF HER APPRECIATION
OF THE POET'S WORK

Kostis Palamas

Kostis Palamas was born on 13th January 1859 in Patras, Greece.

Palamas was educated in Mesolonghi, in Western Greece, before beginning his career as a journalist in the 1880's. Although he had produced many articles, his first publication as a poet was a collection of verse in 1886 under the title *Songs of My Fatherland*.

During his career he published many poetry collections and became one of the most important literary figures in Greece, greatly influencing the political and intellectual climate of his time. His most important poem is his tale of a free-thinking, rebellious intellectual found in his 1907 piece *The Twelve Lays of the Gypsy*. Many consider his work to be some of the finest to come out of Europe, a feeling which was captured with his two nominations for the Nobel Prize for Literature.

Palamas also put lyrics to a score by Spyridon Samaras to create the Olympic Hymn, first performed at the inaugural Olympic Games in 1896 and still recited today at both the summer and winter games.

As a liberal figurehead, his death in 1943, during the German Occupation, became a major event for the Greek resistance. For the occasion of his funeral, a poem was written and recited by Angelos Sikelianos which resulted in mourners staging a hundred thousand strong protest against the Nazi presence in Greece.

PREFACE

The translations contained in the present volume were undertaken since the beginning of the great war when communication with Greece and access to my sources of information were always difficult and at times impossible. In hastening to present them to the English speaking public before discussing them with the poet himself and my friends in Athens, I am only yielding to the urgent requests of friends on both sides of the Atlantic who have regarded my delay with justifiable impatience. I am thoroughly conscious of the shortcomings that were bound to result from the above difficulties and from the interruption caused by my two years' service in the American army; and were it not for the encouragement and loyal assistance of those interested in my work it would have been impossible for me to bring it at all before the public. My earnest effort has been to be as faithful to the poet as possible, and for this reason I have not attempted to render rime, a dangerous obstacle to a natural expression of the poet's thought and diction. But I hope that the critics will judge my work as that of a mere pioneer. I know there is value in the theme; and if this value is made sufficiently evident to arouse the interest of poetry lovers in the achievements of contemporary Greece I shall have reaped my best reward.

I wish to express my thanks to Dr. Christos N. Lambrakis of Athens for the information which he has always been willing to furnish me regarding various dark points in the work translated; to Mrs. Eveleth Winslow of Washington for many valuable suggestions and criticisms; and above all to Professor Clifford H. Moore of Harvard University for the interest he has shown in the work and the readiness with which he has found time in the midst of his duties to take charge of my manuscript in my absence and to assist in seeing it through the press.

Aristides E. Phoutrides.

Washington, D.C.

July 7, 1919.

INTRODUCTION

- Kostes Palamas, a New World-Poet
- Life Immovable, First Part

TRANSLATIONS

- Life Immovable,—Introductory Poem

FATHERLANDS

- Fatherlands, I-XII
- The Sonnets
- Epiphany
- Makaria
- The Market Place
- Loves
- When Polylas Died
- To Petros Basilikos
- Soldier and Maker
- The Athena Relief
- The Huntress Relief
- A Father's Song
- To the Poet L. Maviles
- Imagination
- Makaria's Death
- To Pallis for his "Iliad"
- Hail to the Rime

THE RETURN

- Dedication
- The Temple
- The Hut
- The Ring
- The Cord Grass Festival
- The Fairy
- Out in the Open Light
- First Love
- The Madman
- Our Home
- The Dead
- The Comrade
- Rhapsody
- Idyl
- At the Windmill
- What the Lagoon Says
- Pinks
- Ruins
- Penelope
- A New Ode by the Old Alcaeus

FRAGMENTS FROM THE SONG TO THE SUN

- Imagination
- The Gods
- My God
- Helen
- The Lyre
- Giants' Shadows

- The Holy Virgin in Hell
- Sunrise
- Double Song
- The Sun-Born
- On the Heights of Paradise
- The Stranger
- An Orphic Hymn
- The Poet
- Krishna's Words
- The Tower of the Sun
- A Mourning Song
- Prayer of the First-Born Men
- Thought of the Last-Born Men
- Moloch
- All the Stars
- Arrows

VERSES OF A FAMILIAR TUNE

- The Beginning
- The Paralytic on the River's Bank
- The Simple Song
- Three Kisses
- Ismene
- Thoughts of Early Dawn
- To a Maiden Who Died
- To the Sinner
- A Talk with the Flowers
- To My Wife
- The Answer
- Thought

- The Sinner
- The End

THE PALM TREE

- The Palm Tree

INTRODUCTION

KOSTES PALAMAS

A NEW WORLD-POET

And then I saw that I am the poet, surely a poet among many a mere soldier of the verse, but always the poet who desires to close within his verse the longings and questionings of the universal man, and the cares and fanaticism of the citizen. I may not be a worthy citizen; but it cannot be that I am the poet of myself alone. I am the poet of my age and of my race. And what I hold within me cannot be divided from the world without.

Kostes Palamas, Preface to *The Twelve Words of the Gypsy*.

Kostes Palamas ... is raised not only above other poets of Modern Greece but above all the poets of contemporary Europe. Though he is not the most known ... he is incontestably the greatest.

Eugène Clement, *Revue des Études Grecques*.

I
THE STRUGGLE

Kostes Palamas! A name I hated once with all the sincerity of a young and blind enthusiast as the name of a traitor. This is no exaggeration. I was a student in the third class of an Athenian Gymnasion in 1901, when the Gospel Riots stained with blood the streets of Athens. The cause of the riots was a translation of the New Testament into the people's tongue by Alexandros Pallis, one of the great leaders of the literary renaissance of Modern Greece. The translation appeared in series in the daily newspaper *Akropolis*. The students of the University, animated by the fiery speeches of one of their Professors, George Mistriotes, the bulwark of the unreconcilable Purists, who would model the modern language of Greece after the ancient, regarded this translation as a treacherous profanation both of the sacred text and of the national speech. The demotikists, branded under the name of [Greek: Malliaroi] "the hairy ones," were thought even by serious people to be national traitors, the creators of a mysterious propaganda seeking to crush the aspirations of the Greek people by showing that their language was not the ancient Greek language and that they were not the heirs of Ancient Greece.

Three names among the "Hairy Ones" were the object of universal detestation: John Psicharis, the well known Greek Professor in Paris, the author of many works and of the first complete Grammar of the people's idiom; Alexandros Pallis, the translator of the Iliad and of the New Testament; and Kostes Palamas, secretary of the University of Athens, the poet of this "anti-nationalistic" faction. Against them the bitterest invectives were cast. The University students and, with them, masses of people who joined without understanding the issue, paraded uncontrollable through the streets of Athens, broke down the establishment of the *Akropolis*, in which Pallis' vulgate version appeared, and demanded in all earnestness of the Metropolitan that he should renew the medieval measure of excommunication against all followers of the "Hairy Ones."

Fortunately, the head of the Greek Church in Athens saved the Institution which he represented from an indelible shame by resisting the popular cries to the end. But the rioters became so violent that arms had to be used against them, resulting in the death of eight students and the wounding of about sixty others. This was utilized by politicians opposing the government: fiery speeches denouncing the measures adopted were heard in Parliament; the victims were eulogized as great martyrs of a sacred cause; and popular feeling ran so high that the Cabinet had to resign and the Metropolitan was forced to abdicate and die an exile in a monastery on the Island of Salamis. It was then that I first imbibed hatred against the "Hairy Ones" and Palamas.

About two years later, I had entered the University of Athens when another riot was started by the students after another fiery speech delivered by our puristic hero, Professor Mistriotes, against the performance of Aeschylus' *Oresteia* at the Royal Theatre in a popular translation made by Mr. Soteriades and considered too vulgar for puristic ears. This time, too, the riot was quelled, but not until one innocent passer-by had been killed. I am ashamed to confess that on that occasion I was actually among the rioters. It was the day after the riot that I first saw Palamas himself. He was standing before one of the side entrances to the University building when my companion showed him to me with a hateful sneer:

"Look at him!"

"Who is it?"

"The worst of them all, Palamas!"

I paused for a moment to have a full view of this notorious criminal. Rather short and compact in frame, he stood with eyes directed towards the sunlight streaming on the marble covered ground of the yard. He held a cane with both his hands and seemed to be thinking. Once or twice he glanced at the wall as if he were reading something, but again he turned towards the sunlight with an expression of sorrow on his face. There was nothing conspicuous about him, nothing aggressive. His rather pale face, furrowed brow, and meditative attitude were marks of a quiet, retiring, modest man. Do traitors then look so human? From the end of the colonnade, I watched him carefully until he turned away and entered the building. Then I followed him and walked up to the same entrance; on the wall, an inscription was scratched in heavy pencil strokes:

"Down with Palamas! the bought one! the traitor!"

At last my humanity was aroused, and the first rays of sympathy began to dispel my hatred. That remorseless inscription could not be true of this man, I thought, and I hurried to the library to read some of his work for the first time that I might form an opinion about him myself. Unfortunately, the verses on which I happened to come were too deep for my intellect, and I had not the patience to read them twice. I was so absolutely sure of the power of my mind that I ascribed my lack of understanding to the poet. Then his poems were so different from the easy, rhythmic, oratorical verses on which I had been brought up. In Palamas, I missed those pleasant trivialities which attract a boy's mind in poetry. One thing, however, was clear to me even then. Dark and unintelligible though his poems appeared, they were certainly full of a deep, passionate feeling, a feeling that haunted my thoughts long after I had closed his book in despair. From that day, I condescended to think of him as of a sincere follower of a wrong cause, as of a sheep that had been led astray.

Years went by. I was no more in Greece. I had come to another country, where a new language, a new history, a new literature opened before me. Here, at last, I began to assume a reasonable attitude towards the question of the language of my old country, and here first I could read Palamas with understanding. Gradually, his greatness began to dawn on me, and, finally, my admiration for him had grown so much that when on April, 1914, I reached Greece as a travelling fellow from Harvard University, I had decided to concentrate my studies during the five months I was planning to spend there upon him and his work. With his work, I did spend many long and pleasant hours. But him I visited only once. The man from whom I had once shrunk as from a monster of evil, now I shunned for fear I had not yet learned to admire in accordance with his greatness. Owing to the urgent demand of an old classmate, Dr. Ch. N. Lambrakis, who knew the poet, I went to see him one April afternoon in his office at the University with my friend and fellow traveller, Mr. Francis P. Farquhar. Mr. Palamas was sitting at his official desk; but as soon as we entered he rose to receive us and then sat modestly in the corner of a sofa. He had changed very little in appearance since the time of the riots, and the more I looked at him the more I recognized the very same image which I had kept in my mind from the first encounter I had with him in the University colonnade ten years before. Perhaps, the furrows of his brow had now become deeper; the white hairs, more numerous. His eyes were still the same fiery eyes penetrating wherever they lit beneath the surface of things and often turning away from the present into the world of thought. His hands moved quietly; his voice was clear and sonant; his words were few and polite. Unassuming in his manner, he seemed more eager to receive knowledge than to talk about himself and his work. He asked us questions about America and its literary life: Is Poe read and appreciated? Is Walt Whitman still popular? He admired them both; he had a great craving for the new; and to read things about America fascinated him. When we rose to leave, we realized that we had been doing the talking, but on both of us the personality of the man, reserved and unobstrusive though he was, had made a deep and lasting impression.

This was the only visit I had with him. But I saw him more than once walk in the streets of Athens and among the plane trees of Zappeion by the banks of Ilissus, or sitting alone at a table of some unfrequented coffeehouse, always far from the crowd. It was only after I had returned to America that I wrote to him for permission to translate some of his works. The answer came laden with the same modesty which is so prominent a characteristic of the man. He is afraid I am exaggerating the value of his work, and he calls himself a mere laborer of the verse. Certainly he has been a faithful laborer for a cause which a generation ago seemed hopeless. But through his faith and power, he has snatched the crown of victory from the hands of Time, and he may now be acclaimed as a new World-Poet.

"The poetic work of Kostes Palamas," says Eugène Clement, a French critic, in a recent article on the poet, "presents itself today with an imposing greatness. Without speaking about his early collections, in which already a talent of singular power is revealed, we may say that the four or five volumes of verse, which he has published during the last ten years raise him beyond comparison not only above all poets of Modern Greece but above all poets of contemporary Europe. Though he is not the most famous—owing to his overshadowing modesty and to the language he writes, which is little read beyond the borders of Hellenism—*he is incontestably the greatest.* The breadth of his views on the world and on humanity, on the history and soul of his race, in short, on all problems that agitate modern thought, places him in the first rank among those who have had the gift to clothe the philosophic idea in the sumptuous mantle of poetry. On the other hand, the vigor and richness of his imagination, the penetrating warmth of his feeling, the exquisite perfection of his art, and his gifted style manifest in him a poetic temperament of an exceptional fulness that was bound to give birth to great masterpieces."

II
LIFE INFLUENCES

Patras

Kostes Palamas was born in Patras sixty years ago. Patras is one of the most ancient towns in Greece, known even in mythical times as Aroe, the seat of King Eumelus, "rich in flocks." It became especially prominent after the reign of Augustus as a centre of commerce and industry. Its factories of silk were renowned in Byzantine times, and its commanding position attracted the Crusaders and the Venetians as a military base for the conquest of the Peloponnesus. The citadel walls that crown the hill, on the slopes of which the modern city descends amphitheatrically into the sea, are remnants of Venetian fortifications. In the history of Modern Greece, it is a hallowed spot; for it was here that on April 4, 1821, the standard of the War of Liberation was first raised before a band of warriors kneeling before the altar of Hagia Laura, while Germanos, the archbishop of the city, prayed for the success of their arms. The view which the city commands over the sapphire spaces of the Corinthian Gulf and the purple shadows of the mountains rising from its waters in all directions are superb, and the sunsets, that evening after evening revel in colors there, are among the most magnificent in Greece. A beauty worthy of life dwells over the vine-clad hills, while the mountain kings that rise about are hoary with age and fame. The eye wanders from the purple-laden cliffs of Kylene to the opal mantles of the sea and from the peaks of Parnassus to the lofty range of Kiona. This is the background of one of Palamas' "Hundred Voices," a collection of short lyrics in the volume entitled *Life Immovable*:

> Far glimmered the sea, and the harvest darkened
> the threshing floors;

I cared not for the harvest and looked not on the threshing floors;
For I stood on the end of the sea, and thee I beheld from afar,
O white, ethereal Liakoura, waiting that from thy midst
Parnassus, the ancient, shine forth and the Nine Fair Sisters of Song.
Yet, what if the fate of Parnassus is changed? What if the Nine Fair Sisters are gone?
Thou standest still, O Liakoura, young and for ever one,
O thou Muse of a future Rhythm and a Beauty still to be born.

To his birth place, the poet dedicates one of his collection of sonnets entitled "Fatherlands" and contained in the same volume. It is the first of the series:

Where with its many ships the harbor moans,
The land spreads beaten by the billows wild,
Remembering not even as a dream
Her ancient silkworks, carriers of wealth.
The vineyards, filled with fruit, now make her rich;
And on her brow, an aged crown she wears,
A castle that the strangers, Franks or Turks,
Thirst for, since Venice founded it with might.
O'er her a mountain stands, a sleepless watch;
And white like dawn, Parnassus shimmers far
Aloft with midland Zygos at his side.

Here I first opened to the day mine eyes;
And here my memory weaves a dream dream-born,
An image faint, half-vanished, fair—a mother.

Missolonghi

But in Patras, the child did not stay long. His early home seems to have been broken up by the death of his mother, and we find him next in Missolonghi, another glorious spot in the history of Modern Greece. It does not pride itself on its antiquity. It developed late in the Middle Ages from a fishing hamlet colonized by people who were attracted by the abundance of fish in the lagoon separating the town from the sea. This lagoon lies across the Corinthian Gulf to the northwest of Patras, hardly an hour's sail from it. Its shallow waters, which can be traversed only by small flat-bottomed dories propelled with poles, extend between the mouths of the Phidaris and the Acheloös, and are studded with small islets just emerging above the face of the lagoon and covered with rushes. Two of these islets, Vassiladi and Kleisova, attained great fame by the heroic resistance of their garrisons against the forces of Kioutachi and Imbrahim, Pashas in the War of Liberation. The town itself is a shrine of patriotism for modern Greeks. For from 1822 to 1826, with its humble walls hardly stronger than fences, it sustained the attacks of very superior forces, and its ground was hallowed by the blood of many national heroes. Just outside its walls lies the "Heroes' Garden" or "Heroön," where under the shadows of eucalyptus and cypress trees, Marcos

Bozzaris, Mavromichalis, the philhellene General Coreman, and Lord Byron's heart are buried. It was during the second siege that Byron died here in the midst of his noble efforts for the freedom of Greece. The fall of the city brought about by famine is the most glorious defeat in the history of the Greek Revolution. The garrison of three thousand soldiers with six thousand unarmed persons including women and children, unwilling to surrender, attempted to break through the Turkish lines. But only one-sixth managed to escape. The rest were driven back and mercilessly cut down by their pursuers. Many took refuge in the powder magazines of the city and waited until the Turks drew up in great numbers; then they set fire to the powder and blew up friends and foes alike. The second sonnet of Palamas' "Fatherlands" is devoted to this lagoon city:

> Upon the lake, the island-studded, where
> The breeze of May, grown strong with sea-brine, stirs
> The seashore strewn with seaweed far away,
> The Fates cast me a little child thrice orphan.
> 'Tis there the northwind battles mightily
> Upon the southwind; and the high tide on
> The low; and far into the main's abyss
> The dazzling coral of the sun is sinking.
> There stands Varassova, the triple-headed;
> And from her heights, a lady from her tower,
> The moon bends o'er the waters lying still.

> But innocent peace, the peace that is a child's,
> Not even there I knew; but only sorrow
> And, what is now a fire—the spirit's spark.

Here then, "the spirit's spark" was first kindled, and here, in the city of his ancestors, the poet was born. The swampy meadows overgrown with rushes and surrounded with violet mountains, the city with its narrow crooked streets and low-roofed houses, the lagoon with its still shallow waters and modest islets, the life of townsmen and peasants with their humbles occupations, passions, and legends, above all, the picturesque distinctness of this somewhat isolated place, secluded, as it seems, in an atmosphere laden with national lore—these were the incentives which stirred Palamas in his quest of song. They have stamped their image on all his work, but their most distinct reflection is found in *The Lagoon's Regrets*, which is filled with memories of the poet's early life in a world he always remembers with affection:

> Imagination flies to hells and stars,
> A witch beguiling, an enchantress strange;
> But ours the Heart remains and binds both life
> And love with the native soil, nor seems to die.
> Peaks, depths, I sought Eurydice of old:
> "What longing moans within me now, new-born?
> Would that I were a fisherman at work,
> Waking thy sleeping waters with my oar,
> O Missolonghi!"

Humble but natural in feeling is the appeal to a friend of his childhood days:

> The peasant's huts in Midfield
> For us, old friend, are waiting:
> Come as of old to eat
> The fresh-made cheese, and taste
> The hard-made loaf of cornbread.
> Come, and drink the milk drawn pure;
> And filled with dew and gladness,
> Stir up the hunger of the youth
> Beside you, buxom lasses.

Here, too, he sings of the "crystal salt that is drawn snow-white from the lake"; of the rain "that always weeps" and of the conquering tides. Here he listens to the whispers of the waves while they murmur with each other with restrained pride; and here over Byron's grave he dreams of the great poet of Greece, who will come to ride on Byron's winged horse. The poems of this collection are short but exquisitely wrought in verse and language, full of life and of feeling. They are especially marked with Palamas' attachment to the little and humble, which he loves to raise into music and rhythm, and for which he always has sympathy and even admiration.

Athens, the Violet-Crowned

Missolonghi nurtured the poet in his youth and led him to the threshold of manhood. But when he had graduated from the provincial "gymnasion," he naturally came to Athens in order to complete his education in the University of that city, the only University in Greece. This brought him to the place which was destined to develop his greatness to its zenith. The quiet, retired, and humble life of the Lagoon with its air filled with legend was suddenly exchanged for the shining rocks of Attica and its great city, flooded with dazzling light and roofed with a sky that keeps its azure even in the midst of night. Life here is full, restless, and tumultuous as in the days of Athens of old. The violet shadows of the mountains enclosing the silver olive groves of the white plain are still the makers of the violet crown of Athens.

The poet in one of his "Hundred Voices" pictures a clear Attic afternoon in February:

> Even in the winter's heart, the almonds are ablossom!
> And lo, the angry month is gay with sunshine laughter,
> While to this beauty round about a crown you weave,
> O naked rocks and painted mountain slopes of Athens.
> Even the snow on Parnes seems like fields in bloom;
> A timid greenish glow caresses like a dream
> The Heights of Corydallus; white Pentele smiles upon
> The Sacred Rock of Pallas; and old Hymettus

stoops
To listen to the love-song of Phaleron's sea.

It is its scanty vegetation that makes the southwestern region of Attica look like a mountain lake of light. The nakedness of the mountain ranges and the whiteness of the plains are vaulted over by a brilliant sky and surrounded by a sea of a splendid sapphire glow. Even the olive trees, which still grace the fields about Athens are bunches of silver rather than of green. In "The Satyr, or the Naked Song," taken from the volume of *Town and Wilderness* we may detect the very spirit which, springing from the same soil thousands of years ago, created the song which gradually rose from primitive sensuousness to the heights of the Greek Tragedy:

All about us naked!
All is naked here!
Mountains, fields, and heavens wide!
The day reigns uncontrolled;
The world, transparent; and pellucid
The thrice-deep palaces.
Eyes, fill yourselves with light
And ye, O Lyres, with rhythm!
Here, the trees are stains
Out of tune and rare;
The world is wine unmixed;
And nakedness, a mistress.
Here, the shade is but a dream;

And even on the night's dim lips
A golden laughter dawns!
Here all are stripped of cover
And revel lustfully;
The barren rock, a star!
The body is a flame!
Rubies here and things of gold,
Priceless pearls and things of silver,
Scatter, O divinely naked Land,
Scatter, O thrice-noble Attica!
Here manhood is enchanting,
And flesh is deified;
Artemis is virginity,
And Longing is a Hermes;
And here, and every hour,
Aphrodite rises bare,
A marvel to the Sea-Things,
And to the world, a wonder!
Come, lay aside thy mantle!
Clothe thee with nakedness,
O Soul, that art its priestess!
For lo, thy body is thy temple.
Pass unto me a magnet's stream,
O amber of the flesh,
And let me drink of nectar drawn
From Nakedness Olympian!
Tear thy veil, and throw away
Thy robe that flows discordantly!
With nature only match thy form,
With nature match thy plastic image.
Loosen thy girdle! Cross

Thy hands upon thy heart!
Thy hair is purple royal,
A mantle fairly flowing.
And be a tranquil statue;
And let thy body take
Of Art's perfection chiseled
Upon the shining stone;
And play, and sing, and mimic
With thoughtful nakedness
Lithe beasts and snakes and birds
That dwell in wilderness.
And play, and sing, and mimic
All things of joy, all things of beauty;
And let thy nakedness
Pale into light of living thought.
Forms rounded and forms flat,
Soft down, lines curved and straight,
O shiverings divine,
Dance on your dance of gladness!
Forehead, and eyes, and waves
Of hair, and loins, ...
And secret dales and places!
Roses of love and myrtles!
Ye feet that bind with chains!
Hands, Fountains of caress,
And Doves of longing sweet,
And falcons of destruction!
Whole hearted are thy words,
And bold, O mouth, O mouth,
Like wax of honey bees,
Like pomegranates in bloom.

Life Immovable - First Part

The alabaster lilies,
April's own fragrant censers,
Envy thy breast's full cups!
Oh, let me drink from them!
Drink from the rosy tinged,
Erect, enameled, fresh,
The milk I dreamed and dreamed
Of happiness. Thee!
I am thy mystic priest,
And altars are thy knees;
And in thy warm embrace
Gods work their miracles!
Away, all tuneless things!
Hidden and covered things, away!
Away, all crippled, shapeless things,
And things profane and strange!
Erect and naked all, and guileless,
Bodies and breasts and earth and skies!
Nakedness, too, is truth,
And nakedness is beauty!

* * * * *

In nakedness, with sunshine graced,
That fills the Attic day,
If thou beholdest stand before thee
Something like a monster bare,
Something that like a leafless tree
Stands stripped of shadow's grace,
And like a stone unwrought,
His body is rough and gaunt,

Something that naked, bare, and nude
Roams in the thrice-wide spaces,
Something whose life is told in flames
That light beneath his eyelids,
Akin to the old Satyrs' breed
And tameless like a beast,
A singer silver-voiced,
Flee not in fear! 'Tis I!
The Satyr! I have taken here
Roots like an olive tree,
And with my flute deep-sounding,
I make the breezes languish.
I play and lo, all things are mated,
Love giving, love receiving.
I play and lo, all things are dancing,
All: Men and beasts and spirits!

Athens, the Centre of Greece

So much of the natural atmosphere of Athens and Attica. But the Athenians themselves, their thoughts, life, and dreams have not proved less important nor less effective for the poet's growth. The spiritual and intellectual currents moving the Greek nation of today start from this city. Here politics, poetry, and philosophy are still discussed in the old way at the various shops, the coffee houses, and under the plane trees by the banks of Ilissus. The "boulé" is the centre of the political activity of the state. The University with its democratic faculty and still more democratic student body is certainly a "flaming" hearth of culture. Only, its flames are sometimes so ventilated by current events and political developments that the students often assume the functions of the old Athenian Assembly. In the riotous expression of their temporary feelings, the students are not very different from the ancient demesmen. In my days, at least, the most frequent greeting among students was "How is politics today?", with the word "politics" used in its ancient meaning. Any question of general interest might easily be regarded as a national issue to be treated on a political basis. Thus it happened that when the question of language was brought to the foreground by Pallis' vernacular translation of the New Testament, the students took up arms rather than argument.

Into this world, the poet came to finish his education. In one of his critical essays (*Grammata*, vol. i), he tells us of the literary atmosphere prevailing in Athens at that time, about 1879. That year, Valaorites, the second great poet of the people's language, died, and his death renewed with vigor the controversy that had continued even after the death of Solomos, the earliest great poet of Modern Greece. The passing away of Valaorites left Rangabes, the relentless purist, the monarch of the literary world. He was considered as the master whom every one should aspire to imitate. His language, ultra-puristic, had travelled leagues away from the people without approaching at all the splendor of the ancient speech. But the purists drew great delight from reading his works and clapped their hands with satisfaction on seeing how near Plato and Aeschylus they had managed to come.

Young and susceptible to the popular currents of the literary world, Palamas, too, worshipped the established idol, and offered his frankincense in verses modelled after Rangabean conceptions. In the same essay to which I have just referred, he tells us of the life he led with another young friend, likewise a literary aspirant, during the years of his attendance at the University. The two lived and worked together. They wrote poems in the puristic language and compared their works in stimulating friendliness. But soon they realized the truth that if poetry is to be eternal, it must express the individual through the voice of the world to which the individual belongs and through the language which the people speak.

This truth took deep roots in the mind of Palamas. His conviction grew into a religion permeated with the warmth, earnestness, and devotion that martyrs only have shown to their cause. Believing that purism was nothing but a blind attempt to drown the living traditions of the people and to conceal its nature under a specious mantle of shallow gorgeousness, he has given his talent and his heart to save his nation from such a calamity. In this great struggle, he has suffered not a little. When the popular fury rose against his cause, and he was blackened as a traitor and a renegade, he wrote in words illustrating his inner agony:

> I labored long to create the statue for the Temple
> Of stone that I had found,

To set it up in nakedness, and then to pass;
To pass but not to die.
And I created it. But narrow men who bow
To worship shapeless wooden images, ill clad,
With hostile glances and with shudderings of fear,
Looked down upon us, work and worker, angrily.
My statue in the rubbish thrown! And I, an exile!
To foreign lands I led my restless wanderings;
But ere I left, a sacrifice unheard I offered:
I dug a pit, and in the pit I laid my statue.
And then I whispered: "Here, lie low unseen and live
With things deep-rooted and among the ancient ruins
Until thine hour comes. Immortal flower thou art!
A Temple waits to clothe thy nakedness divine!"
And with a mouth thrice-wide, and with the voice of prophets,
The pit spoke: "Temple, none! Nor pedestal! Nor light!
In vain! For nowhere is thy flower fit, O maker!
Better for ever lost in these unlighted depths.
"Its hour may never come! And if it come, and if
Thy work be raised, the Temple will be radiant
With a great host of statues, statues of no blemish,
And works of thrice-great makers unapproachable.
"To-day was soon for thee; to-morrow will be late.
Thy dream is vain; the dawn thou longest will not dawn;
Thus, burning for eternities thou mayest not reach,
Remain, Cloud-Hunter and Praxiteles of shadows!

"To-morrow and to-day for thee are snares and seas.
All are but traps for drowning thee and visions false.
Longer than thy glory is the violet's in thy garden!
And thou shalt pass away; hear this, and thou shalt die!"
And then I answered: "Let me pass away and die!
Creator am I, too, with all my heart and mind;
Let pits devour my work. Of all eternal things,
My restless wandering may have the greatest worth."

The same idea, though expressed in a more familiar figure, is found in another poem published among *The Lagoon's Regrets*.

The Guitar

In the old attic of the humble house,
The guitar hangs in cobwebs wrapped:
Softly, oh, softly touch her! Listen!
You have awaked the sleeping one!
She is awake, and with her waking,
Something like distant humming bees
Creeps far away and weeps about her;
Something that lives while ruins choke it.
Something like moans, like humming bees,
Thy sickened children, old guitar,
Thy words and airs. What evil pest,
What blight is eating thine old age!

In the old attic of the humble house,
Thou hast awaked; but who will tend thee?
O Mother, wilderness about thee!
Thy children, withering; and something,
Like humming bees, sounds far away!

A distinct note of pessimism is found in the lines of both these poems. In the latter, it becomes a helpless cry of anguish. But despair seems to cure the poet rather than drown his faith in hopelessness. As a critic, he encourages every initiate of the cause. As a "soldier of the verse," he himself fights his battles of song in every field. In short story, in drama, in epic poetry, and above all in lyrics, he creates work after work. From the *Songs of my Country*, the *Hymn to Athena*, the *Eyes of my Soul* and the *Iambs and Anapaests*, he rises gradually and steadily to the tragic drama of the *Thrice Noble-One*, to the epic of *The King's Flute*, and to the splendid lyrics of *Life Immovable* and *The Twelve Words of the Gypsy* which are his masterpieces.

Nor does he always meet adversity with songs of resignation. At times, he faces indignantly the hostile world with a satire as stinging as that of Juvenal. He dares attack with Byronic boldness every idol that his enemies worship. Often he strikes at the whole people with Archilochean bitterness and parries blow for blow like Hipponax. At times, he even seems to approach the rancor of Swift. But then he immediately throws away his whip and transcends his satire with a loftier thought, a soothing moral, a note of lyricism, and above all with an unshaken faith in the new day for which he works. The eighth and ninth poems of the first book of his "Satires" are good illustrations of this side of his work:

8

The lazy drones! The frogs! The locusts!
Big men! Politicians! Men who draw
Their learning from the thoughtless journals!
A crowd of stupid, haughty blockheads!
Unworthily, thy name is set
By each as target for blind blows;
But forward still thy steps thou leadest,
Up toward the high bell-tower above,
And climbest: Spaces spread about thee,
And at thy feet, a world of scorners.
Though thou rainest not the godsent manna,
A great Life-giver still, thou tollest
With a new bell a new-born creed.

9

Aye! Break the tyrant's hated chains!
But with their breaking go not drunk!
The world is always slaves and lords:
Though free, chain-bound your life must be;
Other kinds of chains are there
For you: Kneel down! For lo, I bring them!
They fit you, redeemers or redeemed!
Bind with these chains your golden youth;
I bring you cares and sacrifices.

And you shall call them Truth and Beauty,
Modesty, Knowledge, Discipline!
To one command obey last, first,
The world's great laws, and men, and nations.

One of his "Hundred Voices" has something of this satiric note. It is a blow against a worthless pretender of the art of verse, who courts popularity with strains not worthy of the sacred Muse. Palamas, acting with greater wisdom than Pope, does not give the name of this unknown pretender:

Bad? Would that thou wert bad; but something worse thou art:
Thou stretchedst an unworthy hand to the sacred lyre,
And the untaught mob took thy reeling in the dust
For the true song of golden wings; and thou didst take
Thy seat close by the poet's side so thoughtlessly,
And none dared rise and come to drag thee thence away.
And see, instead of scorning thee, the just was angry;
Yet, even his verse's arrow is for thee a glory!

The Grave

In tracing the great life influences of our poet, we must not pass over the loss of his third child, "the child without a peer," as he says in one of his poems addressed to his wife, "who changed the worldly air about us into divine nectar, a worthy offering to the spotless-white light of Olympus." To this loss, the poet has never reconciled himself. The sorrow finds expression in direct or covert strains in every work he has written. But its lasting monument was created soon after the child's death. A collection of poems, entitled *The Grave*, entirely devoted to his memory, is overflowing with an unique intensity of feeling. The poems are composed in short quatrains of a slowly moving rhythm restrained by frequent pauses and occasional metrical irregularities, and thus they reflect with faithfulness the paternal agony with which they are filled. They belong to the earlier works of the poet, but they disclose great lyric power and are the first deep notes of the poet's genius. A few lines from the dedication follow:

> Neither with iron,
> Nor with gold,
> Nor with the colors
> That the painters scatter,
> Nor with marble
> Carved with art,
> Your little house I built
> For you to dwell for ever;
> With spirit charms alone
> I raised it in a land
> That knows no matter nor
> The withering touch of Time.
> With all my tears,
> With all my blood,

I founded it
And built its vault....

In another poem, in similar strains, he paints the ominous tranquility with which the child's birth and parting were attended:

Tranquilly, silently,
Thirsting for our kisses,
Unknown you glided
Into our bosom;
Even the heavy winter
Suddenly smiled
Tranquilly, silently,
But to receive you;
Tranquilly, silently,
The breeze caressed you,
O Sunlight of Night
And Dream of the Day;
Tranquilly, silently,
Our home was gladdened
With sweetness of amber
With your grace magnetic;
Tranquilly, silently,
Our home beheld you,
Beauty of the morning star,
Light of the star of evening;
Tranquilly, silently,
Little moons, mouth and eyes,
One dawn you vanished
Upon a cruel deathbed;

> Tranquilly, silently,
> In spite of all our kisses,
> Away you wandered
> Torn from our bosom;
> Tranquilly, silently,
> O word, O verse, O rime,
> Your witherless flowers
> Sow on his grave faith-shaking.

In another poem reminiscent of Tibullean tenderness, the corners of the deserted home, in which the child, during his life, had lingered to play, laugh, or weep, converse with each other about their absent guest:

> Things living weep for you,
> And lifeless things are mourning;
> The corners, too, forlorn,
> Remember you with longing:
> "One evening, angry here he sat,
> And slept in bitterness."
> "Here, often he sat listening
> Enchanted to the tale."
> "Here, I beheld with pride
> The grace of Love half-naked;
> An empty bed and stripped
> Is all that now is left me."
> "I always looked for him;
> He held a book; how often
> He sat by me to read
> With singing tongue its pages!"

"What is this pile of toys?
Why are they piled before me
As if I were a grave?
Are they his little playthings?
"The little man comes not;
For death with early frost
Has nipped his little dreams
And chilled his little doings."
"His little sword is idle,
And here has come to rest."
"And here his little ship
Without its captain waits."
"To me, they brought him sick
And took him away extinguished."
"They watered me with tears
And perfumed me with incense."
"The dead child's taper burns
Consuming and consumed."
"The tempest wildly beats
Upon the doors and windows,
And deep into our breasts
The tempest's moan is echoed."
And all the house about
For thee, my child, is groaning ...

The World Beyond Greece

Greece seems to encompass the physical world with which Palamas has come in contact. He does not seem to have travelled beyond its borders, and even within them, he has moved little about. With him scenery must grow with age before it speaks to his heart. Fleeting impressions are of little value, and the appearance of things without the forces of tradition and experience behind it does not attract him:

> Others, who wander far in distant lands may seek
> On Alpine Mountains high the magic Edelweis;
> I am an Element Immovable; each year,
> April delights me in my garden, and the May
> In my own village.
> O lakes and fiords, O palaces of France and shrines
> And harbors, Northern Lights and tropic flowers and forests,
> O wonders of art, and beauties of the world unthought,—
> A little Island here I love that always lies before me.

We must not think, however, that the spirit of Palamas rests within the narrow confines of his native land. On the contrary, it knows no chains and travels freely about the earth. He is a faithful servant of "Melete," the Muse of contemplative study, a service which is very seldom liked by Modern Greeks. In his preface to his collection of critical essays entitled *Grammata* he rebukes his fellow countrymen for this: "On an old attic vase," he says, "stand the three original Muses, the ones that were first worshipped, even before the Nine, who are now world-known: Mneme, Melete, Aoide—Memory, Study, Song. With the first and last, we have cultivated our acquaintance; and never must we show any contempt for the fruit of our love for them.

Only with the middle one, we are not on good terms. She seems to be somewhat inaccessible, and she does not fill our eyes enough to attract us. We have always looked, and now still we look, for what is easiest or handiest. Is that, I wonder, a fault of our race or of our age? And is the French philosopher Fouillée somewhat right when in his book on the *Psychology of Races* he counts among our defects our aversion to great and above all endless labors?" That Palamas is not subject to this fault, one has only to glance at his works to be convinced. There is hardly an important force in the world's thought and expression whether past or present, to which Palamas is a stranger. The literatures of Europe, America, or Asia are an open book for him. The pulses of the world's artists, the intellectual battles of the philosophers, the fears and hopes of the social unrest, the religious emancipation of our day, the far reaching conflict of individual and state, in short, all events of importance in the social, political, spiritual, literary, and artistic life are familiar sources of inspiration for him. With all, he shows the lofty spirit of a worshipper of greatness and depth wherever he finds them. Tolstoi or Aeschylus, Goethe or Dante, Ibsen or Poe, Swinburne or Walt Whitman, Leopardi or Rabelais, Hugo or Carlyle, Serbian Folk Lore or the Bible, Hindu legends or Italian songs, Antiquity or Middle Ages, Renaissance or Modernity, any nation or any lore are objects worthy of study and stores of wisdom for him. Indeed, very few living poets could be compared with him in scholarship and learning.

Nor does he lift his voice only for individual or national throbbings. He sings of the great and noble whenever he sees it. One of his best lyric creations is a song of praise to the valor of the champions of Transvaal's freedom, his "Hymn to the Valiant," the first of the collection entitled "From the Hymns and Wraths," a paean that has been most highly lauded by Professor D.C. Hesseling of the University of Leyden (*Nederlandsche Spectator*, March, 1901). Here is a fragment of it, the words which the Muse addresses to the poet:

> ... Awake! Thou art not maker of statues!
> Awake! For songs thou singest!
> And song is not for ever
> The heart's lament
> To fading leaves of autumn,
> Nor the secret speech thou speakest,
> A Soul of Dream, to the shadows of Night.
> For suddenly there is a clash and groaning!
> The joy of birds sea-beaten,
> In storms of Elements
> And storms of Nations!
> Song is, too,
> The Marathonian Triumpher!
> Over the ashes of Sodoma,
> It is blown by the mouth of wrath!
> Something great and something beautiful,
> Something from far away,
> Travelling Glory brings thee
> On her sky-wandering pinions.

Glory has come! On her wings and on her feet,
Signs of her wanderings are shown,
Dust gold-loaded and distant;
And she brings aloes blossoming, first-seen,
From the land that feeds the Kaffir's flocks.
In your aged summers,
A new-born spring has spread!
From North to South,
The Atlantic Dragon groans a groan first-heard;
To the African lakes and forests,
His groan has spread and echoed;
From the Red Sea, a Lamia's palace,
To the foam-shaped breast of the White Sea,
A Nereid's realm.
Thinly the plants were growing
On the bosom of the ancient Motherland;
Winds carried away the seed
And brought it to the Libyan fields
And scattered it into deep ravines
And on the lofty mountain lawns.
A new blood filled the herbs,
And even the strong-stemmed plants
Waxed stronger.
Men war-glad are risen!
And the waterfalls roar
In the mountain's heart;
Men war-glad are risen
Like diamonds rare to behold
That the earth begets!
You know them, heights, winds, horizons,
High tides and murmurings of restless waters,

Golden fountains, that shall become
Their crowns!
And you, O gold-built mountain passes,
Castles fit for them, you know them;
Their fame, thou heraldest with pride
From thy verdant distant country
To Europe Imperial,
O Africa, O slave unknown!
And first of all thou knowest,
O heartless tamer of continents and races,
Rider of Ocean's Bucephaluses,
Thou knowest the worth of the few,
Who dare live free ...

Within the limits of a general introduction it would be difficult to enter every nook and corner of the poet's world. We must even pass over some of the most potent influences of his life. The national dreams of the Modern Greeks have a splendid dwelling in the thought of Palamas, who follows with restlessness his people's woes and exults in their joys. A group of poems dedicated to the "Land that Rose in Arms" and published in the last volume of the poet's work, the *Town and Wilderness*, form his noblest patriotic expression. The present world-conflict has naturally stirred him to new compositions, of which his "Europe" is preëminently noteworthy as illustrating faithfully the various aspects of the poet's genius. This poem appeared first in the *Noumas*, an Athenian periodical, and was then published in the last volume of the poet's works, the *Altars*.

Europe

I. THE WAR

Deer-like the East pants terror-struck! The West,
A flame ablaze that leaps amid the skies!
Nations are wolves! and Hatreds are afoot,
Whetting their bayonets!

With force gigantic, lo, the bursting forth
Of the barbarian sweeps on, age-wrought;
Oceans are cleft and swallow Gorgon-ships,
Castles of might afloat!

What sorcerers, in Earth's deep bosom buried,
Beat into shape the metal? For what kings
Slave they? What crowns forge they? The tower-ships,
The ports, the oceans quake!
Lovingly the dream born of dream flies high
Air wandering amid the eagles; yet
O victory! Lord of the azure, man
Spreads horror even there.

Methinks the Niebelungen of the Night
Startle sun's radiance ... And ye, the Rhine's
Water-born Nymphs, are lashed and swept away
By monstrous hurricanes.

Siegfried, the hero of the golden hair,
Makes men and elements before him kneel.

War is the arbiter of rising worlds;
And Violence, arbitress.

Franks, Anglo-Saxons, Alemanni, Hungars!
Europe, a viper! And the armies, dragons!
Here, Uhlans are destroyers pitiless;
And there, the Cossacks' bands!

From endless sweeps of steppes, the Slav blows forth
An endless squall, the havoc's ruthless vow!
Liberty is the phantom; and the slave,
The stern reality.

Helvetians, Scandinavians, Latins, Russians,
The martyr Pole, heroic Flanders' land,
All, small and great, forward to battle rush
With one man's violence!
Beating thy breast, thou clingest to thy throne,
Storm-wrapped, O worshipper of gods that fade,
Hypatia thou, the Frenchman's ruling queen,
Blood-bred Democracy!

The Vosgic towers tremble! And God's wrath,
Valkyrie, the awful Nymph, wind-ridden sweeps,
A rider pitiless that threatens thee,
O Paris noble-born!

Our age's honored prophet, Tamerlan!
A shadow's dream, Messiah of sweet Peace!

Enthroned in judgment stands America.
While from far Asia's depths,

The Indian hermits and gold-gatherers
With yellow Mongols are afoot! With them,
The sons of Oceania, Kerman,
And Africa; Semites,

War-glad Turanians and Aryans,
Lands that the Adriatic kisses, Rumans,
Our brother Serb, a wall!—Let Austria's
Cataract burst and roar!

Vosges and Carpathians and Balkans quake!
Ridges and mountains tremble! The oceans roar!
Five Continents' passionate wraths and hatreds
Revel in festival!

But lo, the Briton with sea-battling sceptre
That binds the restless waves to his command—
What Caesars' fetters forges he anew
Upon the island rock?

And there the Turk, who holds thee with dog's teeth
And makes of thee a valley of sad tears,
O paradisial land of old Ionia;
And here, our Mother Greece,

Dream-weaver of unending laurel-wreaths
Beside her Cretan helmsman and her king!

Wax-pale, the world stands listening and holds
Its breath, benumbed with fright!

II. THE THINKER

But lo, the thinker, whatever is his soul,
Whatever race has given him his blood,
Watches from his unruffled haunts calm-wrapped
And he stirs not.

With pity's quivering and terror's chill,
In tears and ruins, he plucks a fruitful joy
From the great Drama, watching thoughtfully
The hidden law.

And lo, the thinker, whatever is his soul,
Whatever race has given him his blood,
Abides in his unruffled haunts calm-wrapped
And meditates:

Old age? No! Nor the youth of a new life.
All is the same, Europe and Law, the shark!
And never changes—hear ye not?—the march
Of history.

A splinter in the powerful's hands, O powerless,
Yet sometimes—comfort thee—his mate and
friend!
The powerful's blind hand even thou, O Science,
Often shalt be.

Is War the Father of all things? And is
The lava messenger of lusty growth?
How can the creature grow from monster seed?
Who knows? Pass on!

Even if some great dream be born of flesh
And the wroth tempest fling a new world forth,
Even if over the tumult Europe stand
United, one;

And if the state of a new people rise
Founded upon the ruins of the world,
Still always thou wilt burn, O Fury's torch,
Amid the darkness.

Even if thou wilt come to states in ruins
And empty thrones, O power of juster race,
Always the tender and the harsh shall be;
Shepherd and flocks!

Unless, O man, something is destined thee
That thou, O History, foretellest not:
An evolution unbelievable
To gazing worlds.

III. THE POET

The poet: Miracle-working lo, the seed
Of blessed dreams, sown in his heart, takes roots;

He is like mind entranced in ecstasy,
Born upon wings!

Under his wings, all things are images
Of creatures beautiful for him to sing,
Whether they are roses April-born
Or warring legions!

And neither the war's roaring gun nor yet
The river of red blood swift-flowing on
Can make the flower fade that fills my breast
With fragrances!

I am the faithful friend of song; therefore,
I tremble not like child before a blackman;
Midst blood and flames and lashings horrible,
I bring thee, Love!
Thy footprints mark a shining trail of lights
New-risen, guiding with their gleams my steps;
The restless gambol of thy fire, Dawn's smile
Upon my night.

Thine eyes, O Fountainhead of Beauty's stream,
Mirror within them all things beautiful:
And lo, the eagles of the Czars, on wings
Sky-roaming, sail.

The war, when thine eyes look on it, becomes
Under the magic of thy glance pure wine
Of holiness. The German is the wonder
Of deed and thought;

Where Tolstoi lived, all things are justly blessed;
Where Goethe dwelt all things are light and
wisdom;
And yet my heart's pure love flows now for thee,
For thee, O France!

Though first I sucked my god-sprung mother's
milk,
Still thou wert later manna unto me,
Desert-born, joy of mine and guide and teacher,
My second mother.

On thy world-trodden earth, I have not stood;
Nor didst thou bathe me, Seine, in thy cold waters;
Yet is thy vision light unto my song,
O second mother!
O Celtic oak-trees and Galatian-born
White lilies in lyric Paris blossoming,
With Hugo and with thee, O Lamartine,
Revels and wings!

Dante and Nietzsche, Ibsen, Shakespeare, all,
Poured wine for me with their thrice-holy hands
Into thy gleaming cup of gold and bade
Me rise on high.

A child: And thou didst flash before me first,
Tearing the maps of dazzled Europe's lands
With the world's Mirabeaus and with the world's
Napoleons.

Thou art not for the gnawing worm of graves.
Thy gods still live with thee, Hypatia!
Glory and Victory may dwell with thee,
Democracy!

From the number of the life influences which we have scantily traced in Palamas' work we may conclude that he is a true representative of the great world and of the age in which he lives. Loving and true to his immediate surroundings, he does not localize himself in them, nor does he shut his thought within his personal feelings and experiences, but he travels far and wide with the thought and action of the universal man and fills his life with the life of his age.

It is exactly this universalism that makes *The Twelve Words of the Gypsy* his best expression and at the same time the most difficult to understand thoroughly. The poem is reflective both of the growth of the poet himself and of the development of the human spirit throughout the ages with the history and land of Hellas as its natural background. Consequently, its message is both subjective and objective. Although differently treated, the theme is the same as that of the "Ascrean" which appears in the latter part of *Life Immovable* and which may be considered as a prelude to *The Twelve Words of the Gypsy*. There is a flood of feeling and a cosmic imagery throughout, but they only form the gorgeous palace within which Thought dwells in full magnificence and mystic dimness. "As the thread of my song," says the poet in his preface, "unrolled itself, I saw that my heart was full of mind, that its pulses were of thought, that my feeling had something musical and difficult to measure, and that I accepted the rapture of contemplation just as a lad accepts his sweetheart's kiss. And then I saw that I am the poet, surely a poet among many—a mere soldier of the verse, but always the poet who desires to close within his verse the longings and questions of the universal man and the cares and fanaticism of the citizen. I may not be a worthy citizen. *But it cannot be that I am the poet of myself alone; I am the poet of my age and of my race; and what I hold within me cannot be divided from the world without.*"

Washington, D.C.

July 5, 1919.

LIFE IMMOVABLE

FIRST PART

In Palamas, we have found every trait of the Greek character: He is religious and superstitious; a skeptic, a pagan, and a pantheist.... He is a poet and a philosopher.... He abandons himself to every impulse of the Greek soul. But he is always fond of drawing back, of concentrating, of trying to encompass in a general form the sensations and ideas which sway him. His principal and latent care is to analyze himself and his world. A poet and a thinker, Palamas does not attract the multitudes.... With him everything is a mingling of lights and shadows.... But through his work Greece of today is most clearly set forth.

Tigrane Yergate, "Le Mouvement litteraire grec; La Poesie." *La Revue*, June, 1903, vol. xlv, p. 717 f.

With *Life Immovable*, the poetic genius of Kostes Palamas reaches its full strength. The poet, who, from his very first work, *The Songs of my Country*, had shown his power in selecting his sources of inspiration and in weaving the essence of purely national airs into his "light sketches of sea and olive groves and the various sunlit aspects of Greek life," continues to broaden his vision and art through an unquenchable eagerness for knowledge, for an understanding of things beautiful, whether present or past, concrete or abstract. He makes broad strides from his *Hymn to Athena*, to *The Eyes of My*

Soul, Iambs and Anapests, and *The Grave.* In all "the pathetic and the common meet inseparably with an art exact and full of grace, an art that knows its purpose." But in *Life Immovable* Palamas rises above the Hellenic horizon, and strikes the strings of the universal heart in the same degree as the towns of Patras, Missolonghi, and Athens expand into Greece and Greece into the world. After all there is both realism and symbolism in the fact that the first poem of the volume reflects the atmosphere of the poet's native town while one of the latter ones "The Ascrean" is filled with an all-including world-vision.

The present volume contains only the first half of *Life Immovable.* It consists of five collections of poems: The "Fatherlands," "The Return," "Fragments from the Song to the Sun," "Verses of a Familiar Tune," and "The Palm Tree." On the whole, a careful study of these collections would furnish the key to an adequate understanding of the rest of the poet's works for which these poems are faithful preludes. For this reason I am tempted to give an analysis of the translated parts as a guide to their understanding. But it is by no means my wish to lay down a fast rule; poetry is no exact science and there should be always ample room for freedom of suggestion and of view.

1. Fatherlands

A series of sonnets, the "Fatherlands," make the opening of the book and, at the same time, symbolize most clearly the growth of our poet. Each sonnet describes a fatherland, adding another link to a chain of worlds that dawn, one after another, upon the poet's being. The first is Patras, his birthplace. Then follows Missolonghi with its calm lagoon and the haunts of his boyhood. The splendor of the violet-crowned city of Athens is succeeded by the island of Corfu, the cradle of the literary renaissance of Modern Hellenism, which again fades before the vision of Egypt, whence the earliest lights of civilization shone upon the land of the Greeks. Christianity in its extreme form of asceticism is brought forth from one of its strong citadels, Mt. Athos, the holy mountain of Greece, and a contrast is made between the "gleaming beauties of the world" and the utter absorption of the ascetic by the intangible world beyond. The vision of "Queen Hellas," the classic age of Greece, is followed by the conquering spirit of Hellenism spreading triumphantly from the democracies of Athens and Sparta to the Golden Gate of imperial Byzantium.

But "imagination, like the Phaeacians' ship, rolls on," and the poet sings:

> In my soul's depths loom many lands ...
> And where the heavens mingle with the sea,
> A path I seek for a sphere beyond ...

Oceans are crossed, ages are brought forth from the past, and continents are joined in making the poet's spirit. Finally even Earth becomes too narrow and the greater universe opens its gates to the ultimate fatherland, the elements of the world which will at the end absorb the being of the poet:

> Fatherlands! Air and earth and fire and water,
> Elements indestructible, beginning
> And end of life, first joy and last of mine,
> You I shall find again when I pass on
> To the grave's calm. The people of the dreams
> Within me, airlike, unto air shall pass;
> My reason, firelike, unto lasting fire;
> My passions' craze unto the billows' madness.
> Even my dust-worn body, unto dust;
> And I shall be again air, earth, fire, water;
> And from the air of dreams, and from the flame
> Of thought, and from the flesh that shall be dust,
> And from the passions' sea, ever shall rise
> A breath of sound like a soft lyre's complaint.

2. The Return

The second collection of *Life Immovable*, entitled "The Return," is dedicated to the poet's country. It bears under its title the significant date of 1897, the year of the unfortunate Greco-Turkish war which ended disastrously for Greece and plunged the nation into despair. After the defeat, almost the whole world spoke of the Greeks as of a degenerate people beyond the hope of redemption. The sensitiveness of the race helped in rendering the gloom of disaster most depressing. For some time, even the Greeks began to resign themselves to their fate as a hopeless one. Palamas is one of the first to sound the reveille. He conceives of his collection of songs as an expression of faith in the country's future. With perfect love and assurance "he comes to place the crowns of Art" "dream-made and dream-engraved" upon her shattered throne....

> Only with harmony sublime and pure,
> Which, though it rises over time and space,
> Turns the world's ears to his native land,
> The poet is the greatest patriot.

Nevertheless even the poet's spirit cannot help reflecting the gloom through which it tries to rise. The general depression about him weighs upon him, too, in spite of his effort. This shadow haunts him constantly. Life becomes a Fairy, with a Fairy's dangerous charms and fearful mysteries. "Something like a madman pursues life." The poet hears this madman's falling steps and is horror-haunted:

> And lo, blood of my blood the madman was!
> A past, ancestral, long-forgotten sin,
> That bursting forth upon me, vampire-like,
> Snatched from my hand the dewy crown of joy!

This madman grows from within the individual's and the nation's life. The wings of joys and dreams are clipped. One feels like a night-owl upon glorious ruins, the beauty of which makes the night even darker. Tradition, like a majestic temple, seems to choke life by its solemnity. The present, which seems to be symbolized by the little hut, is in the relentless grip of "a monstrous vision, the Fairy Illness, stripped in the silver glimmer of the moon." There is always the mingling of gleaming beauty and of bitter sorrow. There is always before us a "cord-grass festival," the amber fragrant flowers budding upon the piercing spikes of the cord-grass and luring man to the deadly bog where there is no redemption. One might say that the poet verges on morbidity.

But such an assumption would be unjust. Palamas may have a clear vision of the tragedy of life. But in the light of this revelation, with his unfettered contemplation, he builds, like Bertram Russell, a "shining citadel in the very centre of the enemy's country, on the very summit of his highest mountain; from its impregnable watch-towers, his camps and arsenals, his columns and forts, are all revealed; within its walls, the free life continues while the legions of Death and Pain and Despair and all the servile captains of tyrant Fate afford the burghers of that dauntless city new spectacles of beauty." In like manner, the world of Greece, in which Palamas lives, "our home," as he calls it, may have its dreadful silences that are "full of moans," moans vague and muffled as if coming from a distant world

Of bygone ages and of times unborn.

But he does not lose sight of that

> Harmony fit for the chosen few, ...
> A lightning sent from Sinai and a gleam
> From great Olympus, like the mingling sounds
> Of David's harp and Pindar's lyre, conversing
> In the star-spangled darkness of the night.

At times the poet even raises his song to rapture. Certainly the past becomes a source of happiness in his "Rhapsody," and life is agleam with joy in his "Idyl." But most reflective of this power of the poet to conquer darkness with light and to turn ruins into gleaming palaces of beauty and of song, is the poem entitled "At the Windmill."

The local color which is by no means a rare characteristic of the poetry of Palamas is particularly rich in this collection. Many of its songs are vivid and clear pictures of Greek life. Yet with the touch of symbolism, he makes such local flashes world-flames. In "The Dead," we have a faithful description of the Greek custom of exposing the open coffin with the body in a room whence all furniture is removed. Friends and relatives are gathered about the dead; even children are not excluded from paying this last honor to the departed. The windows are closed, and in the gloom tapers and candles are burning before the images of the saints and over the flower-covered body, while the smoke of the incense and the fragrance of the wreaths fill the air. Yet somehow in the verses of the song one catches the moving sounds of mourning humanity, the image of death against life.

3. Fragments from the Song to the Sun

"The Fragments from the Song to the Sun" contain some of the noblest lines of Palamas' poetry. We cannot have a complete understanding of the symbolism with which this part of *Life Immovable* is filled. For, after all, from the great hymn to the light-god, we have here only fragments. But these fragments remind one of the gold-stained ruins of the *Akropolis* against the bright Attic sky. Throughout, we are aware of a striking duality. The key to these sunlit melodies is probably found in the "Giants' Shadows." Among the shadows whose voices ascend from darkness "like moanings of the sea," the poet discovers Telamonian Ajax, the giant who is utterly absorbed in the world within him, the source of his light and life, and Goethe, the Teutonic poet, who turns to the world about himself as a flower to the sun, and whose heart "longs and thirsts for light." Here then, we detect the doubleness of the sun of Palamas, a sun within, the source of his inner life and thought, and a sun without, the source of all external beauty and growth.

Thus without detracting from the charm and power of the day-star, he ensouls it with a higher meaning and transforms a fiery globe into a light-clad Olympian divinity, a giver of life and death, a healer and a slayer. In "The Tower of the Sun," we find mighty princes, sons of kings, who had gone thither in their desire to hunt for the light, turned into stones by the "giant merciless." Motionless they stand, a world of voiceless statues while

> From their deep and smothered eyes,
> Something like living glance
> Struggles to peep through its stone-veil!

Then the fair redeemer, a princess beautiful, comes from far away—the light, it seems, of inner knowledge and inspiration—and the Sun's tower

> Gleamed forth as if the light
> Of a new dawn embraced its walls!

She knows where the fountain of life flows and with its waters wakes up the sons of kings, shining

> ... with transcending gleam
> Like a far greater Sun.

This is, then, the sun whom Palamas worships as a god. It is a sun who possesses all the beauty and power of the actual source of light, but who, at the same time, by the spell of mystic symbolism rises to the splendor of a thrice-fair and almighty divinity containing all that is beautiful and noble and powerful in the world. Upon such a sun he seeks to find a light-flooded palace for his child in the "Mourning Song." To such a sun he offers his hymns and prayers; and such a sun he conceives as a vengeful blood-fed Moloch or a muse of light. He is a fair Phoebus, who rises from pure Olympus' heights to play as a fountain of flowing harmonies or to smite as "an archer of fiery arrows" all living things.

4. Verses of a Familiar Tune

In the "Verses of a Familiar Tune" the poet conceives of himself as of a wedding guest who travels far away to join the festival. The bride, "thrice-beautiful" seems to be Earth; and the bridegroom, the Sun. The journey to the festival is the span of mortal life. The poet, who must travel over this path, endeavors to brighten it with dreams and shorten his way's weary length

> With sounds that like sweet longings wake in him
> Old sounds familiar, low whisperings
> Of women's beauties and of home-born shadows ...
> The flames that burn within the heart, the kisses
> That the waves squander on the sandy beach,
> And the sweet birds that sing on children's lips!

The second poem of this group, "The Paralytic on the River's Bank," recalls the notes verging on despair which we have found in "The Return." Again the gleaming past, appearing here as the other bank of the river, revels

> In lustful growth and endless mirth
> With leafy slopes and forests glistening.

At the sight of such splendor, the poet lies palsy-stricken on this bank of the river, the "graceless, barren, and desert bank" unable to rise and sing. Then Life, like a merciful Fairy, takes him into the humble hut of the present and makes him forget the other bank and nourishes him until, at last, waking into the new world, he weaves the whole day long with master hand all kinds of laurel crowns and pours into the unaccustomed air a flute's soft-flown complaint. But again from his bed he raises his eyes and sees once more the world beyond the river, nodding luringly at him; and even there, in the midst of the new life, he falls palsy-stricken, "the paralytic of the river bank."

This note of hopelessness is immediately counteracted by the "Simple Song," in which Life opens again her gorgeous gardens of the past to pluck the fairest of flowers; and when he weeps over the newly reaped blossoms that fill his basket, Life rebukes him by facing them unmoved "a life agleam!" With like wholesomeness he greets the early dawn that brings him "thought, light, and sound, his sacred Trinity," and enters the chapel's garden

> To see the children beautiful,
> Children that make the grassy beds a heaven
> And rise like miracles among the flowers.

But on the whole, man, the wedding guest, must travel on while the winds of uncertainty blow about him. Riddles face him everywhere; questions stern and unanswerable spring before him; and the life of the whole human race seems to be that of Thought likened to "an angel ever wrestling with a strong giant flinging his hundred hands about the angel's neck to strangle him." For who knows if a good act unknown shines more than the most splendid monuments of marble or verse? Who knows if vice is wiser than virtue? Is Fair Art, War's Triumphs, and great Thoughts expressed costlier in the Temple of the Universe than the mute Thought and Glory of the flower,

> ... at whose birth
> The dawn rejoices and whose early death
> The saddened evening silently laments?
>
> The thoughtful sage high-rising smites the gates
> Of the Infinite and questions every Sphinx;
> Yet who knows if the soldier with no will,
> Obeying blindly, is not nearer Truth?
>
> O struggle vast! Who knows what power measures
> The measureless and creates the great?
> Is it the matchless thought of the endowed,
> Or the dim soul of the multitude that bursts,
> Thoughtless of reason, into life? Who knows?

We know not "whether the holy man's blessing" is the best, nor whether there is more light of Truth in the Law, "that is all eyes," or in some blind love. Thus entangled in the meshes of life's sphinx-like wonders, we spend our day, little particles of the great world-struggle, wedding guests at Life's strange festival!

5. The Palm Tree

In tenderness and delicacy of thought and expression, no part of *Life Immovable* can be compared with the smoothly flowing stanzas of "The Palm Tree." There is no ruggedness in the meter, no violence in the stream of images. We are led without knowing it into a modest garden. A few flowers, a palm tree, some bushes, and the sky make our world, a world, it seems, of things small and common and trivial. But the poet passes by, listens to the humble flowers of dark and light blue, and puts their talk into rhythms.

At once, the flowers become a world of beauty, life, and thought. They are our kin, sons of the same parent Earth, and dreamers of strangely similar dreams. The Palm tree over them becomes a great mystery of power and grace lifting it to the realm of gods. The flowers, like little mortals, wonder at the things they see about them. Their own existence beneath the palm tree's shade is full of riddles, and they face the world with questionings. In the very midst of a clear sky's festival that succeeds a rain, the little flowers suffer the first blows of pain, dealt by the last drops that fall from the palm leaves, and they feel the agony of sorrow until they come to realize that even pain brings its reward, knowledge, which makes them glory, like victors, over death. Their being expands and they sing a song which is the essence of the world's humanity:

Though small we are, a great world hides in us;
And in us clouds of care and dales of grief
You may descry: the sky's tranquility;
The heaving of the sea about the ships
At evenings; tears that roll not down the cheeks;
And something else inexplicable. Oh,
What prison's kin are we? Who would believe it?
One, damned and godlike, dwells in us; and she is
Thought!

Thus their song continues carrying them from thought to thought, from dream to dream, from joy to joy, and from sorrow to sorrow. Swept away by the charms of life, they raise to their strange god a hymn of exultation. At the sight of the thrice-fair rose, they sing a song of love and admiration. Their experiences stimulate their minds, and they seek to solve the dark problems that teem about them. With the eagerness of living beings they listen to the tales of new worlds and miracles brought to them by bees and lizards. Illness and night frighten them with fearful images; and, at last, they pass away with a song of hope and regret:

We shall die,
Nor will there be a monument for us
That might retain the phantom of our passing!
Only about thee will a robe of light
Adorn thee with a new and deathless gleam:
And it shall be our thought, and word, and rime!
And in the eyes of an astonished world,

Thou wilt appear like a gold-green new star;
Yet neither thou nor others will know of us!

Harvard University,

June 3, 1917.

TRANSLATIONS

LIFE IMMOVABLE

INTRODUCTORY POEM

And now the columns stand a forest speechless
And motionless; and among them, the rhythms
And thoughts move in slow measures constantly;
   And in their depths, light-written images
Show Love that leads and Soul that follows him.

From the "Thoughts of Early Dawn."

I labored long to create the statue for the Temple
On stone that I had found
And set it up in nakedness; and then to pass;
To pass but not to die.
And I created it. But narrow men who bow
To worship shapeless wooden images, ill-clad,
With hostile glances and with shudderings of fear,
Looked down upon us, work and worker, angrily.
My statue in the rubbish thrown! And I, an exile!
To foreign lands, I led my restless wanderings.
But ere I left, a sacrifice unheard I offered:
I dug a pit; and in the pit I laid my statue.
And then I whispered: "Here lie low unseen and live
With things deep-rooted and among the ancient ruins
Until thine hour comes. Immortal flower thou art!
A Temple waits to clothe thy nakedness divine!"

And with a mouth thrice-wide, and with the voice of prophets,
The pit spoke: "Temple, none! Nor pedestal! Nor light!
In vain! For nowhere is thy flower fit, O Maker!
Better forever lost in the unlighted depths!
"Its hour may never come! and if it come, and if
Thy work be raised, the Temple will be radiant
With a great host of statues, statues of no blemish,
And works of thrice-great makers unapproachable!
"Today, was soon for thee; tomorrow will be late!
Thy dream is vain! The dawn thou longest will not dawn;
Thus burning for eternities thou mayest not reach,
Remain cloud-hunter and Praxiteles of shadows!
"Tomorrow and today for thee are snares and seas!
All are but traps for drowning thee and visions false!
Longer than thy glory is the violet's in thy garden!
And thou shalt pass away—hear this!—and thou shalt die!"
And then I answered: "Let me pass away and die!
Creator am I, too, with all my heart and mind!
Let pits devour my work! Of all eternal things,
My restless wandering may have the greatest worth!"

FATHERLANDS

To the blessed shade of Tigrane Yergate who loved my Fatherlands.

I

Where with its many ships the harbor moans,
The land spreads beaten by the billows wild,
Remembering not even as a dream
Her ancient silkworks, carriers of wealth.
The vineyards, filled with fruit, now make her rich;
And on her brow, an aged crown she wears,
A castle that the strangers, Franks or Turks,
Thirst for, since Venice founded it with might.
O'er her a mountain stands, a sleepless watch;
And white like dawn, Parnassus shimmers far
Aloft with midland Zygos at his side.
Here I first opened to the day mine eyes;
And here my memory weaves a dream dream-born,
An image faint, half-vanished, fair—a mother.

II

Upon the lake, the island-studded, where
The breeze of May, grown strong with sea-brine, stirs
The seashore strewn with seaweed far away,
The Fates cast me a little child thrice orphan.

'Tis there the northwind battles mightily
Upon the southwind; and the high tide on
The low; and far into the main's abyss
The dazzling coral of the sun is sinking.
There stands Varassova, the triple-headed;
And from her heights, a lady from her tower,
The moon bends o'er the waters lying still.
But innocent peace, the peace that is a child's,
Not even there I knew; but only sorrow
And, what is now a fire, the spirit's spark.

III

Sky everywhere; and sunbeams on all sides;
Something about like honey from Hymettus;
The lilies grow of marble witherless;
Pentele shines, birthgiver of Olympus.
The digging pick on Beauty stumbles still;
Cybele's womb bears gods instead of mortals;
And Athens bleeds with violet blood abundant
Each time the Afternoon's arrows pour on her.
The sacred olive keeps its shrines and fields;
And in the midst of crowds that slowly move
Like caterpillars on a flower white,
The people of the relics lives and reigns
Myriad-souled; and in the dust, the spirit
Glitters; I feel it battling in me with Darkness.

IV

Where the Homeric dwellers of Phaeacia
Still live, and with a kiss meet East and West;

Where with the olive tree the cypress blooms,
A dark robe in the azure infinite,
E'en there my soul has longed to dwell in peace
With towering visions of the land of Pyrrhus;
There dream-born beauties pour their flood,
Dawn's mother
Lighting the fountain of sweet Harmony.
The rhapsodies of the Immortal Blind
In the new voice of Greece are echoed there;
The shade of Solomos in fields Elysian
Breathes rose-born fragrance; and master of the lyre,
A new bard sings, like old Demodocus,
The glories of the Fatherland and Crete.

V

Lo, dreams strange-born among my dreams are mingling;
A lake, the ancient Mareotis, where
The Goddess spreads with ever hidden face
Her wedding couch to greet Osiris Lord.
As if from graves, from laughless depths, before me
Life brightly glitters with her gentle smile;
A Libyan thirst burns in my heart; and Ra,
The fiery archer, battles everywhere.
Something sow-like before me gnashed its teeth,
The slavish soul and savage of the Arab;
World-nourishing the Nile rolled on its waters;
And lotus-crowned, in the cool shade of palms,
I loved as beasts that dwell in wilderness
A Fellah lass full-breasted and sphinx-faced.

VI

A sinner hermit on the Holy Mountain,
I burn in Satan's fire and pine in hell;
My soul is ruins and woe; and in a stream
Deep-flowing, I sink, a traveller beguiled.
The blue Aegean spreads a sapphire treasure;
Like Daphnis and his Chloe stand sky and earth;
Quivering, lo, the seed of life blooms forth;
In swarms, the living beings suck the sap
Of all. Olympus, Ossa, Pelion,
And every lap of sea, and every tongue
Of land, lake-like Cassandra, Thrace's shores
Are clad in wedding garb; and I? "O Lord,
Be my Redeemer!" and with floods of tears
I bathe the god-child Panselenus wrought.

VII

Rumele is a royal crown of ruby;
Moreas is a glow of emerald;
The Seven Isles, a jasmine sevenfold;
And every Cyclad, a Nereid sea-born.
Even the chains of rugged Epirus laugh;
And Thessaly spreads far her golden charms.
Hidden beneath her present waves of woe,
Methinks I look on Hellas, Queen of lands.
For still the ancient fir of valor blooms;
And from the pangs and sighs of ages risen,
The breath of Digenes fills all the land
Breeding a race of heroes strong and new;
And in the depths of green and golden Night
Sings on Colonus Hill the nightingale.

VIII

From Danube to the cape of Taenaron,
From Thunder Mountain's End to Chalcedon,
Thou passest now a mermaid of the sea
And now a statue of marble Parian.
Now with the laurel bough from Helicon
And now with sword barbarian, thou sweepest;
And on the fields of thy great labarum,
I see a double headed image drawn.
The sacred Rock gleams like a topaz here;
And virgins basket-bearing, clad in white,
March in a dance and shake Athena's veil;
But far the sapphires shine of Bosporus;
And through the Golden Gate exulting pass
Victors Imperial triumphantly.

IX

Like the Phaeacians' ship, Imagination
Without the help of sail or mariner
Rolls on; in my soul's depths loom many lands:
Thrice-ancient, motionless like Asia,
And others five-minded and bold like Europe's realms;
Despair like Africa's black earth holds me;
Within me a savage Polynesia spreads;
And always I trail some path Columbian.
All monstrous things of life, the fields aflame
Under a tropic sun, I knew; I wore
The shrouds of the poles; and on a thousand paths,

Life Immovable - First Part

I saw the world unfurled before my eyes.
And what am I? Grass on a clod of earth
Scorned eve

X

A traveller, I found in waveless seas
Calypso and Helena thrice-beautiful;
And on the Lotus Eaters' shores, I drank
The blissful waters of oblivion.
In the sun-flooded land, I stood by him,
The god of the Hyperborean race;
One night—in strange and peerless radiance—
The Magi showed to me the mystic star.
I saw the Queen of Sheba on her throne,
O Soul, light flowing from her fingers' touch;
My eyes beheld Atlantis Isle, that seemed
An Ocean flower beyond a mortal's dreams;
And now the care and memory of all
These things are rhythm to me and verse and song.

XI

About the chariot of the Seven Stars,
Sky-racers numberless, whole worlds of giants
And beasts: Ocean of suns, the Milky Way,
Orion, and the monsters of the spheres—
The fearful Zodiac. The Lion roars
Amidst the wilderness ethereal;
The Lyre plays; and trophy-like, the Lock
Of Berenice gleams; and rhythms and laws

Fade in the space of mysteries. Sun, Cronus,
Mars, Earth, and Venus sweep in swift pursuit
Towards the world magnet of great Hercules.
Only my soul like polar star awaits
Immovable, yet filled with dreamful longings;
And knows not whence it comes nor where it goes.

XII

    Fatherlands! Air and earth and fire and water!
Elements indestructible, beginning
And end of life, first joy and last of mine!
You I shall find again when I pass on
    To the graves' calm. The people of the dreams
Within me, airlike, unto air shall pass;
My reason, fire-like, unto lasting fire;
My passions' craze unto the billows' madness;
    Even my dust-born body, unto dust;
And I shall be again air, earth, fire, water;
And from the air of dreams, and from the flames
    Of thought, and from the flesh that shall be dust,
And from the passions' sea, ever shall rise
A breath of sound like a soft lyre's complaint.

THE SONNETS

From their foreign land and precious,
From their nest in green, I took
Red-plumed birds; and then I closed them
In a cage of woven gold.

And the cage of woven gold
Then became a second nest;
On our shores the birds have found
A new, precious fatherland.
Softly here they shake their feathers;
Swiftly sing of worlds and souls
Deep and spacious; or they mingle
Lightning-like their tears and smiles.
And though small and as of coral,
Yet they sing with accents loud.

1896.

EPIPHANY

With chariot drawn by star-plumed peacocks, lo,
The goddess of desires before her people
Is revealed! She passes on, youth's joyful shout
And torture, dragging my eighteen years behind.
Snowflakes became a world; and, taking life
As substance, made her body and her thought.
Upon her royal brow, birds strange and wild,
Scorn's breed, have built their nest and there abide.
Upon her path, in vain I build the palace
Of virgin dreams with virgin gold for her,
Raising a throne of diamonds in its midst.
She passes on her starlit chariot;
And as if filled with golden dreams divine,
She does not even look upon my palace!

1895.

MAKARIA

To you, who dawned before me, offspring of
The great abyss and flower of foaming billows!
To you, whom with their love all things embrace,
And who stir tempests in a statue's depths!
To you, O woman and O virgin, myrrhs,
Fruit, frankincense, I offer recklessly!
To you, the music of the world! To you,
My songs' pure foam, songs that your vision fills!
For you can love, remember, understand.
Before I saw you in the world's great night,
You shone upon my mother's lighted face.
Your worshipper into the world I came;
Your name I knew not, and in love's sweet font
I called you with the name *Makaria*!

1895.

THE MARKET PLACE

Just as dry summers pant for the first rain,
So thou art thirsty for a happy home
And for a life remote, like hermit's prayer,
A corner of forgetting and of love.
And thirsty for the ship upon the sea
That ever onward sails with birds and sea-things,
Filling its life with our great planet's light.
But unto thee both ship and home said: "No!

"Look neither for the happiness remote
That never moves, nor for the life that ever finds
In each new land and harbor a new soul!
"Only the panting of a toiling slave
For thee! Drag in the market place thy body's
Nakedness, strange to the strangers and thine
own!"

1896.

LOVES

Some people love things modest and things small,
And like to feed in cages little birds;
They deck themselves with garden violets
And drink the singing waters of the brooks.
Others delight in tales told by the embers
Of the home hearth or listen to the songs
Of the nightbirds with rapture; others, slaves
Of a great pain, burn incense to the stars
Of beauty. And some thirst for the forest shades
And for a nacreous dawn, and for a sunset
Dipped in red blood, a barren wilderness
Light-burned. But thee no love with nature binds;
And where the heavens mingle with the sea,
A path thou seekest for a sphere beyond.

1896.

WHEN POLYLAS DIED

With wings and hands ethereal, rhythms and thoughts
Lifted thy soul, redeemed from its dust frame,
And led it straightway to the stars; and there
The sacred escort halts and ends its journey.
In summers paradisiac beyond,
Where on the Lyre's star the bards and makers,
Like doves with breath immortal, dwell in gleams,
The shade of Solomos like magnet draws thee,
And leading thee before a double Tabor,
Thus speaks to thee: "Here is thy glory! Here
Dwell and behold the giant pair that stand
Before thee never setting, with diamonds dark;
And like a breath of worship pass, embracing
Thy Homer and thy Shakespeare, blessed One!"

1896.

TO PETROS BASILIKOS

O bard, whose songs unto the vernal god
Of idyls rang from the same gladsome flute,
April's sweet-breathing air is mingled now
With martial sounds of savage trumpetings.
A crown is woven for our motherland:
Is it life's laurels or the martyr's thorns?
Oh see beyond: the wild vine's flowers now
Are shaken on a lake of blood and tears!

Has the war phantom blown upon thee too?
Or hast thou with the force of lightning winds
Flown where for ages sacred hatreds burn
In flames? Or has an evil wound thrown thee
Upon the earth where now in vain the god
Of idyls tries to raise thee with his kisses?

1897.

SOLDIER AND MAKER

Soldier and maker swiftly I
Seized with my hand the spear and spoke:
"Fall on the beast of the world beyond
And strike the eagle-wingèd lion!"
Before me with God's grace, I saw
Soulless the griffin seven-souled,
Blood spurting from a hole hell-like
And scorching with its heat the grass!
And then restored with calm, I saw
The savage strife like a day's dawn;
And the destroyer, I, became
A maker; and with this same hand,
I carve on ivory the man
Who slew the beast and make him deathless.

1896.

THE ATHENA RELIEF

Why leanest thou on idle spear?
Why is thy dreadful helmet bent
Heavy upon thy breast, O virgin?
What sorrow is so great, O thought,
As to touch thee? Are there no more
Of thunder-bearing enemies
To yield thee trophies new? No pomp
Athenian to guide thy ship
On to the sacred Rock? I see
Some pain holds Pallas fixed upon
A gravestone. Some great blow moves her:
Is it thy sacred city's loss,
Or seest thou all Greece—alas—
Of now and yesterday entombed?

1896.

THE HUNTRESS RELIEF

Whither so light of garb and swift of foot, O Huntress?
Is it the sacred gifts of pure Hippolytus
That make thee leave Arcadia's forest land behind,
O shelter of the pure, and slayer of the wild?
Wild lily of virginity raised on the fields
Olympian, O mountain Queen of gleaming bow,
I envy him who in a careless hour did face
Thy beauty's lightning with thy heartless vengefulness.

And yet white like the morn, thou openest in secret
Thy lips thrice fragrant with divine ambrosia
And sayest: "Latona's deathless grace has moulded me
Under the sacred tree upon Ortygia;
But now once more upon the noble stone, the new
Maker has moulded me with a new deathlessness."

1895.

A FATHER'S SONG

O first-born pride and joy of my own home,
I still remember thy coming's sacred day:
The early dawn was breaking as from pearls,
Whitening the sky that spread star-spangled still;
Thou wert not like the fresh and budding rose
In its green mother's clasp before it opens;
Thou camest like a victim pitiful
And feeble cast by a rude hand among us.
And as if thou wert seeking help, thy wail
Rose sadder than the sound of a death knell;
And thus the last of thy own mother's groans
Was mingled with thy first lament. Life's great
Drama began. I watch it, and I feel
Within me Fear's and Pity's mystic wail!

1894.

TO THE POET L. MAVILES

Thy soul is seeking tranquil paths
Alone; thou hatest barking mouths;
And yet thy country's love enflames thee,
O maker of the noble sonnet.
In the white alabaster vase
Filled with pure native earth, a flower
Of dream that only few can see
Trembles and scatters fragrances.
Thy verse, the vase; thy mind, the flower.
But a hand broke the vase, and now
The azure beauty of the flower
Has found a mate in the powder's smoke
Upon Crete's Isle, the blue sea's crown,
Mother of bards and tyrant slayers.

1896.

IMAGINATION

Time's spider lurks and lies in wait;
And on its poisoned claws, the beast
All watchful glides, assails, and grasps
The ruin. O thrice-holy beauties!
In vain all props and wisdom's arts!
In vain a tribe of sages seek
To save it! Time's remaining crumbs
Are scattered far and melt like frost.

Then from the lofty land of Thought,
Imagination came, a goddess
Among the gods, and made again,
Even where until now the ruin
Crumbled, what only its hands can make—
Deathless the first-born Parthenon.

1896.

MAKARIA'S DEATH

To die for these, my brothers, and myself;
For by not loving my own life too much,
I found the best of finds, a glorious death.

    Euripides, *Herakleidae*, 532-534.

On Athens' earth, Zeus of the Market place
Sees Hercules's children kneeling down
On his pure altar, strange, forlorn, thrice-orphan.
Fearful the Argive sweeps on; duty's hand
Is weak. The king of Athens pities them,
But cruel oracles vex him with fear:
"Lo, from thy blood, thrice-noble virgin, shall
The conquerless new enemy be conquered."
None stirs, alas! Orphanhood is forsaken
By all. Then, filled with pride of heroes, thou,
Redeemer of a land and race, divine
Daughter thrice-worthy of the great Alcides,
Plungest into thy breast the victim's sword
And diest a thrice-free death, Makaria.

1896.

TO PALLIS FOR HIS "ILIAD"

From cups that are both ours and strange,
Enameled, and adorned with leaves
Of laurel and of ivy green,
We quaff the wine both pure and mixed.
The liquid that within us burns,
Or poured in cups about us gleams
And bird-like sings, brings us away
To the far Isle of dreams. But thou
Enviest not the path of dreams,
Nor sharest in our drunken revel;
For with our fathers' spacious cup,
The strong and simple, thou hast brought
Immortal water from the spring
Of Homer, thou O traveller!

1903.

HAIL TO THE RIME

Cyprus's shores have not beheld thee born of foam;
A foreign Vulcan forged thee on a diamond anvil
With a gold hammer; and the bard who touches thee,
Bound with thy magic beauty's charms, remains thy thrall.
The yearning prayers of a lover fondly loved
Cannot accomplish what thou canst, strange

nightingale!
Thy song wafts me upon the tranquil fields of calm
When jackals born of woeful cares within me howl.
Thy might gives even sin a garment beautiful;
And thought divine before thee bows in reverence.
Imagination's ship sails with thy help straight on
Where Solomon and Croesus have their treasuries.
To thee I pray! Answer my greeting lovingly,
Thou new tenth Muse among the nine of old, O
Rime!

1896.

THE RETURN
1897

(1897 is the year of the Greco-Turkish war which ended disastrously for Greece.)

DEDICATION

Mother thrice reverend, O widowed saint,
Upon thy shattered throne I come to place
The crowns of Art, dream-made and dream-engraved.
With war storms desolate, my native land,
Trod by the Turk and by strangers scorned thou wert;
Even thy child beholding thee in ruins,
As if the waters of Oblivion
In dark Oblivion's Dale had touched his lips,
Left thee; and thou didst writhe like a whole world
Engulfed in sounds of woe: Hair-tearings and
Breast-beatings, groans of sad despair, night-bats
Wandering restlessly, unheeded prayers
Of souls condemned, loud thunder peals, fierce glares
Of lightnings, and the laughter of the fiends!

But lo, unknown and humble I, with calm
Upon my countenance and storm in mind,
Far from the panic-stricken market place,
Beneath the plane trees' shade, and far away
By the blood-tinctured settings of the suns,

Unruffled, in another land I travelled,
And deep I dug in distant treasure mines.
And with my hand, that knows no rifle's touch,
Slowly I hammered on the crowns of art;
And if thou findest nowhere on their gleam
Thine image painted, or thy blessed name
Written, thou knowest still, O motherland,
Though in thy woe's abyss they seem unlike,
And though a strange and careless glimmer shines
On them, they were created out of thee;
For thee I made them; and for thee I raised them.

Perhaps, when in the midst of wilderness
And ruins thou first openest thine eyes,
O hapless One, my humble offerings
Will not appear like thy wrath's threats, nor like
The joyful trumpetings of thy reveille,
Nor like an image of thy passion's cross,
Nor like thy sorrow's dirge, nor like glad hymns;
But like soft songs and trembling lights and fondlings
Of lily hands, black birds, and stars unknown.

Thus when, smitten with Charon's knife and sunk
In death's dark swoon, a hapless mother feels
Life's tide return, she hears again, like first
Life-summons, the anxious voice of her fond child,
A voice that comforts her and tenderly
Tells of a thousand tales of love his fancy
Weaves or his memory recalls, and drowns

His faintest sigh not to remind his mother
Of the unerring blow of Charon's knife.

Mother thrice-reverend, O widowed saint,
Upon thy shattered throne I come to place
The crowns of Art dream-made and dream-
engraved.
Though they will echo not thy sorrow's groans,
A child of thine has bound them on thine earth
With gold; upon their circles thine own speech
Is shown with master tongue; their light is drawn
From thy sun's gleaming fountain; seek no more!

Only with harmony sublime and pure,
Which, though it rises over time and space,
Turns the world's ears to his native land,
The poet is the greatest patriot.

THE TEMPLE

My knees, bent on thy marble pavement, bleed,
O Temple built apart in wilderness
For an unseen divinity, a goddess
Who from her being's deep abyss reveals
Only a statue wrought by human hand
And even covered with a veil opaque.
Methinks I see among thy sculptured columns,
Among thy secret treasures and thine altars,
Ion, the Delphic priest, who lays aside

The snow-white raiment of the sacrifice
And takes up the wayfarer's knotty staff.
I am no ministrant, nor have I held
The dreadful mystic key, nor have I touched
Boldly or timidly the sacred gate
That leads to Life's deep-hidden mysteries.
One sinner more, O Temple, in the midst
Of sinful multitudes, I come to worship.
My knees, bent on thy marble pavement, bleed;
I feel the chill of night or of the tomb
Creeping upon me slowly, stealthily.
But lo, I struggle to shake off the evil
That creeps on me so cold; with longing heart,
I drag my bleeding knees beyond thy walls,
Out of thy columns—forests stifling me—
Into the sunlight and the moon's soft glimmer.
Away with prayer's burning frankincense!
Away with the gold knife of the sacrifice!
Away with choirs loud-voiced and clad in white,
Singing their hymns about the flaming altars!
Abandoning thee, O Temple, I return
To the small hut of the first bloom of time.

THE HUT

O humble hut of the first bloom of time,
Neither the noisy city's mingled Babel,
Nor the most tranquil soul of the great plain,
Nor the gold cloud of dust on the wide road,
Nor the brook's course that sings like nightingales,
Nothing of these is either shown to thee

Or speaks before thy bare and flowerless window,
O humble hut of the first bloom of time.
Only the neighbor's step now echoes on
From the rough pavement built in Turkish times;
The black wall's shadow, on the narrow street;
And on the lonely ruins lightning-struck
Ere they became the glory of a house,
The nettles revel lustful and unreaped.
Beneath the bare and flowerless window's sill,
A nest of greenish black, like a small heart,
Hangs tenantless and waits and waits and waits
In vain for the return of the first swallow
That has gone forth, its first and last of dwellers.
O thirsty eyes that linger magnet-bound
On the nest's orphanhood of greenish black!
O ears filled with the terror of the tune
That travels to the bare and flowerless window
High from thy roof moss-covered with neglect,
O humble hut of the first bloom of time!
It is the tune the lone-owl always plays
Blowing upon the cursèd flute of night
Its lingering shrill notes of mournful measure,
Herald of woe and prophet of all ill.

THE RING

The ring is lost! The wedding ring is gone!

A folk song.

My mother planned a wedding feast for me
And chose me for a wife a Nereid,
A tender flower of beauty and of faith.
My mother wished to wed me with thy charms,
O Fairy Life, thou first of Nereids!
And hastily she goes to seek advice,
Begging for gold from every sorceress
And powerful witch, and gold from forty brides
Whose wedding crowns are fresh upon their brows;
And making with the gold a ring enchanted,
She puts it on my finger and she binds
With golden bond my youthful human flesh
To the strange Fairy—how strange a wedding
ring!—
I was the boy that always older grew
With the transporting passion of a pair
Bethrothed who, lured by longing, countenance
Their wedding moment as an endless feast
Upon a bridal bed of lily white.
The boy I was that always older grew
Gold-bound with Life, the Fairy conqueress;
The boy I was that always older grew
With love and thirst unquenchable for Life;
The boy I was that always older grew
Destined to tread upon a path untrod
Amidst the light, illumined. I was he
Whose brow like an Olympian victor's shone
And like the man's who tamed Bucephalus.
I was the nimble dolphin with gold wings,
Arion's watchful and quick deliverer.

But then, one day,—I know not whence and how—
Upon a shore of sunburned sands, the hour
Of early evening saddened with dark clouds,
I wrestled with a strange black boy new-come,
Risen to life from the great sea's abyss;
And in the savage spite of that long struggle,
The ring fell from my finger and was gone!
Did the great earth engulf it? Did the wave
Swallow it? I know not. But this I know:
For ever since, the binding spell is rent!
And Fairy Life, the first of Nereids,
My own bethrothed, that was my slave and queen,
Vanished away like a fleet cloud of smoke!
And ever since, from my first-blooming youth
To the first flakes of silver that now fall
On the black forest of my hair, since then,
Some power dumb and dreadful holds me bound
With a mere shadow fleeting and unknown
That seems not to exist, yet ever longs
And vainly strives to enter into being.
And now I am Life's widowed mate and hapless,
Life's great and careless patient! Woe is me!
And I am like the fair Alcithoe,
Daughter of the ancient king, who changed her form
And as a sign of the gods' vengeful wrath
Is now instead of princess a night-bat!

THE CORD GRASS FESTIVAL

See far away, what a glad festival
The golden grasses on the meadow weave!
A festival thrice-fragrant with blond flowers!
With the sweet sunrise sweetly wakening,
I also wish to join the festival
And, like a treasure reaper, to embrace
Masses of flowers blond and fresh with dew,
And then to squander all my flower treasure
At my love's feet, for my heart's ruling queen.
But the gold-spangled meadow spreads too deep;
And, just as mourning for some dead deprives
A life rejoicing with its twenty years
Of its light raiments of a lily-white,
So is my swift and merry way cut short
By a bad way that lies between, without
An end, beset with brambles and with marshes!
The thorny plants tear like an enemy's claws;
And like bird-lime the bad plain's mire ensnares
My feet among the brambles and the marshes,
Where, in the parching sun's enflaming shafts,
The brine, like silver lightning, strikes my eyes!
Where is the coolness of a breath? Where is
The covering shadow of a leafy tree?
I faint! My frame is bent! My way is lost!
I droop exhausted on the briny earth,
And in my lethargy I feel the thorns
Upon my brow; the bitter brine upon
My lips; the sultriness of the south wind
Upon my hands; the kisses of the marsh
Upon my feet; the rushes' fondling on
My breast; and the hard fate and impotence

Of this bare world within me.
Where art thou,
My love?
See far, in depths of purple sunsets
Gorgeously painted, the glad festival
That golden grasses on the meadow weave,
The festival thrice-fragrant with blond flowers,
Sees me, and calls me still, and waits for me!

THE FAIRY

When in the evening on my hut the moon
Spreads her soft silver nets that dreams have wrought,
The hut is caught, and, by the net bewitched,
It changes and becomes a lofty tower.
And then, unseen by the Day's Sun, the father
Of Health, the rosy-cheeked, who always sees
All things with careless and short-sighted eyes,
A monstrous vision lo, the Fairy Illness,
Stripped in the silver glimmer of the moon,
Herself of moonlight born, looms into sight
Slowly in the enchanted tower's midst!
In whitening shimmers, she, like sea at night,
Advances with the step of sleeping men;
Death's pallor is her own, though not Death's chill;
Her ivory skeleton is mantled by
A fleshy cover made of fiery air;
The uncouth flowers on her dragging veil
Seem, like the poppies, crimson red and black;
And still more uncouth look the countless things

Wrought on its folds: dragons and ogresses,
Fevers and lethargies and pains of heart,
Nightmares and storms and earthquakes, breaking nerves.
Delirium flies from her burning lips,
A language made of odd, discordant rhythms.
To nothing, either hers or strange, her eyes
Are like; deep, as abyss untrod, they yawn,
And seem as if they gaze immovable
On empty space. Yet shouldst thou stoop with thirst
To mirror on her staring eyes thine own,
Then wouldst thou see worlds buried in their caves,
Like ruined cities of whole centuries,
Sunk in the fairy-spangled oceans' depths!

OUT IN THE OPEN LIGHT

Out in the open light, the Sun is shining,
Father of Health, Health rosy cheeked, whose breasts
Are full, and yield their milk abundantly;
She only sees those things of flesh about
Which her divine sun-father shows to her;
And her unconquerable iron hands
Are matched with careless and short-sighted eyes.
Out in the open light, even the moon,
The Sibyl, clothed in white, appears, with glance
Lyncean, piercing deep and bringing forth
From the world's ends great hosts of monstrous

things,
The monsters born of shadows and of dreams.

FIRST LOVE

When in my breast I felt my first-born love,
Thrice-noble maiden of compliant heart,
I was possessed with the strange fear that filled
The youthful princess of the ancient tale
At sight of the black man's enchanted rod.
O mate, who madest first my early years
Blossom, too soon thou fleddest far from me
Nor sawest me again! Wild Fairies took
My speech, and evil demons seized my all;
Yet soul and body, my whole being shivers
From that awakening thou sangest me,
Eternal Woman! Thou wert what far Mecca
Is for the faithful's prayer to his prophet.
O far off Mecca! O eternal Fear
Of white Desire upon the shining wings
Of a black sinner! O king Love, chased like
Orestes, by a Fury serpent-haired!

THE MADMAN

A madman chased my early childhood years
Thrice-sweet and blossoming, and seizing them—
Alas!—he crushed them in his reckless fury
Like twigs of purple-colored pomegranate!
He scattered them in pieces everywhere:
Into the joyless house and in the yard,

On narrow streets, and paths, and pathless haunts,
Where persecution raves, and menace dumb
Chills all away from the pure light and air.
The madman's cursed hands hold everything
With snares and claws and stones and knives; they fall
On loneliness and on embracings, night
Or day, on sleep or wake, and everywhere!
And yonder on the streets and in the houses,
Children like me in age, whose years were filled
With bloom and sweetness, freely ran and laughed
And played. Behind me, close, the madman's snares
I heard; and then, the deadened sound of feet!
I breathed his flaming breath! And if his steps
Were slow, still wilder did his laughter hunt me!
Oh, for my life's cold quiverings of pain!
Oh, for the goading—not like the divine
Goading that drove the maid of Inachus,
Io, to wander on and on in frenzy;—
But like the sudden goading that smites down
The little bird when first it tries its wings!
And lo, blood of my blood the madman was!
A past, ancestral, long forgotten sin,
That, bursting forth upon me vampire-like,
Snatched from my head the dewy crown of joy!

OUR HOME

Our home has not the ugly clamoring
Nor the dumb stillness of the other homes

About and opposite. For in our home
Rare birds sing forth uncommon melodies;
And in our home-yard a young offshoot grows,
Sprung from Dodona's tree oracular!
And in the garden of our home, full thick,
The ironworts and snakeroots blossom on;
And in our home the magic mirror shines
Reflecting always in its gleaming glass
The visage of the world thrice-wonderful!
The silence of our home is full of moans,
Moans vague and muffled from a distant world
Of bygone ages and of times unborn;
And in our home souls come to life and die.
Blossom from blossom blossoms forth and fades!
Old men have the white, rich, Levitic beard,
The foreheads wide of solemn contemplation,
The wrath of prophets, and the fleeting calm
And chilling threatfulness of the gray shadows.
Glowing with love-heat like resistless Satyrs,
The young men in the mind's most shady glades
Hunt ardently the bride that is pure thought.
The children drop their playthings carelessly,
And, standing in a corner motionless,
Open their eyes in thought like men full-grown.
And all, ancestors and descendants, young
Or old, have ways that challenge ridicule
And have the word that bursting forth makes slaves!
But still more beautiful and pure than these,
An harmony fit for the chosen few
Fills with its ringing sounds our dwelling place,

A lightning sent from Sinai and a gleam
From great Olympus, like the mingling sounds
Of David's harp and Pindar's lyre conversing
In the star-spangled darkness of the night.

THE DEAD

Within this place, I breathe a dead man's soul;
And the dead man, a blond and beardless youth!
A youthful light and blond stirs in our home;
And moments fly, and days and years and ages.
The dead man's soul is in this lonely house
Like bitter quiet about a calm-bound ship
That longs for the sea-paths, and dreams of storms.
All faces, smoked with the faint smoke that glides
From candles lighting death! All eyes, still fixed
On a sad coffin! And the mute lips, tinged
With the last kiss's bitterness, still tremble.
As for a prayer, hands are raised, and feet
Move quietly as behind a funeral.
The snow-white nakedness of the cold walls
And black luxuriance of the mourning robes
Are like discordant music of two tunes.
The children's step is light in thoughtful care
Lest they disturb the slumber of the dead.
The old men, bent as at a pit's dark end,
Lean on the virgins' shoulders, virgins fair
Like fates benevolent and comforting.
The young men seek on endless paths to find
In Wisdom's hands the weed Oblivion.
And on the window shutters that are closed,

The clay pots with their flowers seem to be
A dead man's wreath; and the lone ray that glides
Through the small fissure is transformed within
Into a taper's light on All Souls' Day.
The candle burning at the sacred image
Is flickering and snaps as if it wrestled
With death. At moments, led astray, comes here
A butterfly of varied wings and brings
In airy flesh the *Ave* of the soul
That did enchant the house, the house that seems
Glad for its dead yet loves and longs for him,
The dead blond youth, and claims him as its own!
And luring him, that it might hold for ever
Its chosen love relentlessly, it has
Now changed its form and turned from house to grave!

THE COMRADE

O boy of the glad school of seven years,
With thy tall form, a shadow of all thou wert.
Thy voice had sweetness never heard before,
A font of holy water of which all
Partook with fear and longing! We forgot
With thee the book and laughed thy merry laughter;
Thou didst tear lifeless readings from our minds
Together with the pedant's torpid mullen,
And didst sow deep into our hearts the seed
Of the gold tree that dazzles with its light,
And charms, and is a tale most wonderful!

The princesses, with valiant heroes mated,
Shone in the hauntless palace of our thought,
First-born; and on imagination's meadow,
Another April bloomed. We saw Saint George,
The rider, slay the dragon and redeem
The maiden. They were not letters that thy hand's
White clay did write, but like the mystic seal
Of Solomon, it scratched a magic knot;
And thy forefinger moved within thy hand
Like fair Dionysus' thyrsus blossoming!
Amidst the restless swarm of humming children,
We had the clamor; and thou hadst the honey,
Turning attention to a prayer, thou,
O comrade of the early years that bloomed,
O chosen being, unforgettable,
Worthy of everlasting memory!
Wherever thou still art or wanderest;
Whomever thou hast followed of the two
Women, who, in the past, did stir Alcmena's
Great son, after thou camest upon them
On some crosspath; whether thou blossomest
Like the pure lily, or tower-like thou risest;
Whether thou art neglected like a crumb,
Shinest as thy country's pride, or art alone,
A stranger among strangers wandering;
Whether life's riddle or the grave's holds thee;
Whatever and wherever thou now art,
O brother mine and mate, from my lips here
Accept my distant kiss with godlike grace!

RHAPSODY

Homer divine! Joy of all time and glory!
When in the coldness of a frigid school,
Upon the barrenness of a hard bench,
My teacher's graceless hands placed thee before me,
O peerless book, what I had thought would be
A lesson, proved a mighty miracle!
The heavens opened wide and clear in me;
The sea, a sapphire sown with emerald;
The bench became a throne palatial;
The school, a world; the teacher, a great bard!
It was not reading nor the fruit of thought:
A vision it was that shone most wonderful,
A melody my ears had never heard.
In the great cavern that a forest deep
Of poplars and of cypresses encircles,
In the great fragrant cavern that the glow
Of burning cedar beats with pleasant warmth,
Calypso of the shining hair spins not
Her web with golden shuttle; nor sings she
With limpid voice. But lifting up her hands,
She pours her curses from her flaming heart
Against the jealous gods:
"O mortal men
Adored by the immortal goddesses,
Who on Olympus shared with you their love's
Ambrosia, and mortals crushed to dust
By jealous gods!..."
The goddess's awful curse
Makes the fresh celeries and violets fade,

And, like the hail sent by the heaven's wrath,
It burns the clusters on the fruitful vines!
The hero far renowned of Ithaca
Alone heeds not the flaming curse, that he,
A wanderer, in the Nymph's heart did light
Unwittingly. But sea-wrecked and sea-beaten,
He sits without, immovable, with eyes
Fixed far away; and thus remembering
His native island's shores, for ever weeps
Upon the coast and near the sea thrice-deep.
The white sea-gull that often in its flight
Plunges its wings into the brine to catch
The fish, and the lone falcon perched afar
In the deep forest, lonely and remote,
Listen and answer to the hero's wail.
Oh, for my phantasy's revealed first vision!
Oh, for the baring of the beautiful
Before me! Lo, the dusty, dark-brown land
Changes into a Nymph's isle lily-white!
The humble fisher lass upon the rock,
Into Calypso of the shining hair, love-born!
My heart, a traveller into a thousand
Lands, thirsting for one country, which is love!
And lo, my soul is, ever since, a lyre
Of double strings that echoes with its sound
The harmony thrice ancient, curse or wail!
Joy of all time and glory, godlike Homer!

IDYL

Now when the tide has covered all the land,
Making the pier a sea, the street a strand,
And the boat casts anchor at my threshold;
Now when I see, wherever I may glance,
The water's victory, the billow's glory,
And see the rising tide a ruling empress;
Now when a playful and good-minded flood
Closes about the houses, plants, and men
Fondly, in a soft-flowing, sweet embrace;
Now when the air, the planter of the tree
Of Health, raised by the great sea's breath, digs deep
Into the open breasts of living things;
Now, I remember her, the little lass
Who had the sea's pure dew, and, like a wave
Resistless, surpassed the tide in vehemence.
Now I recall the little nimble lass,
Life's victory, blossoming youth's proud glory,
And joy's own throne. Now I remember her.
Her face was like a cloudless early dawn;
Her hair like moonlight shimmering upon
The restless wave; her passing, like the flash
Of a swift fish that in the night swims by
Upon its silver path; her eyes were tinged
With the deep color of the sea beneath
Black clouds; her voice, the sound of a calm night
Upon the beach; her chiseled dimples twin
Upon her cheeks were overfilled with smiles

That Loves might drink from them to slake their
thirst.
Boy-like, she stepped on nimble foot and free,
Boldly and daringly with fearless look,
A child's soul dwelling in a woman's flesh.
And when the high tide covered all the land,
Making the pier a sea, the street a strand,
And when the boat cast anchor at my threshold,
Then from her home the little girl came forth
Half bare, half clad, robed in the robe of light
In a swift dancing flood that revelled full
Of water-lust and crowns of seething foam.
She gave her orders to the sea; she ruled
The tide and forward drove the foaming waves,
Just as a shepherd lass, her white-clad sheep.
Her native country, first and last, the sea!
And whenever she passed, a Venus new
Seemed rising from the shining water's depths.
The fisherman, a primitive world's breed,
The sum of Christian and of Satyr blood,
Returning from his fruitful fishing path,
Looked upon her as on an evil tempter
And on a sacred image; and his oars
Hung on his hands inert as palsy stricken,
And the swift-winging bark stood like a rock;
And, marble-like, the fisherman within
Gazed with religious trembling and desire,
Exclaiming as in trance: "O holy Virgin!"

AT THE WINDMILL

About the windmill, the old ruin, when
The smile of dawn shines in its rosy tinge,
The fisherboys now stir the silent air
With sudden ringing shouts and joyful plays;
And the light barks that, fastened, wait their coming,
Flutter impatiently like flapping wings
Of birds whose feet are bound. And all about,
The lake-like sea revels in shimmers white
Like a wide-open pearl shell on the beach.
About the windmill, the old ruin, when
The noon's beams burn like red-hot iron bars,
A laden sleep draws with its heavy breath
All weary skippers and all mariners:
The harpoons creak not in the hand's hard clasp;
The fish alone stir in the realm of dew;
The calm lagoon about is all agleam,
A shield of silver, plaited with pure gold.
Far by the windmill, the old ruin, when
The sun is setting, decked in all his glory,
The boys go running, looking for pumice stones;
And lads and lasses, for sweet furtive glances;
And old men, lingering for memories.
Old age is calm, and youth considerate.
And the lagoon about, a purple glow,
A garden thickly planted with blue gentians.
Far by the windmill, the old ruin, when
The secret midnight glides by silently,
Sea Nereids, brought on the wings of air

From the sea caves of Fairies on their steeds
Of mist with manes of radiating light,
Sing songs, and bathe their diamond forms, and love,
While round about the princess-like lagoon
Wears as her royal robe the star-spun sky.
Far by the windmill, the old ruin, ere
The smile of dawn shine with its rosy tinge,
The hosts of tyrant slayers mount from below
And kiss the earth war-nurtured and war-glad.
They raise again the ruin to a castle
With rifles singing back to victories;
And the lagoon is full of flashes swift,
Like a dark eye kindled with fiery wrath.

WHAT THE LAGOON SAYS

I have the sweetness of the lake and have
The bitterness of the great sea. But now,
Alas! my sweetness is a little drop;
My bitterness, a flood. For the cold winter,
The great corsair, has come with the north wind,
Death's king. My azure blood has slowly flowed
Out of my veins and gone to bring new life
To the deep seas. A shroud weed-woven wraps me.
My little islands as my tombstones stand,
And yonder well-built weirs are like young trees
That droop above my grave bereft of water.
But even so in the death's cold clasp, I hear
Within my breast a secret voiceless flutter
Like the young fish's flurry when, transfixed,

It is dragged by the spear out of the sea.
For I still dream of the sweet breath of love,
And wait for the hot summer's kiss and yours,
O angels of good tidings and new life,
Spring breezes, sources of my dreams and love!

PINKS

Fair pinks, with your breath, I have drunk your soul!
Brown is the fisherman, and brown the land
With the sea brine, the south wind, and the sun;
And round the brown land's neck, like necklace
Of coral, grow the pinks. Pinks of the gardens,
And pinks of the windows; pinks like crowns and stars;
Gifts good for any hand, and ornaments
For any breast. O flowers blossoming
In pleasant rows along the houses' stairs,
You sprinkle each man's path with fragrances;
And now and then, you bow, touched by the dress
Of the young girl who, breeze-like, passes by.
Pinks full and pinks faint-colored; flowers that cause
No languor as the roses nor refresh,
Like jasmines, flesh and soul; but whose scent has
Something of the sharp breath of the lagoon,
Even when you are pale like fainting virgins,
And even when a world-destroying fire
Enflames your petals without burning you!

Pinks, that display now your form's nakedness
Like children's bodies freshly bathed, and now
The varied ornaments of senseless dwarfs,
And now the purple of great emperors!
All the transporting music of the red,
Like that of many tuneful instruments,
Springs from your heart and knows no end, but plays
Before my eyes its lasting harmonies.
Sweet pinks, with your breath, I have drunk your soul!

RUINS

I turned back to the golden haunts of childhood,
And back on the white path of youth; I turned
To see the wonder palace built for me
Once by the holy hands of sacred Loves.
The path was hidden by the thorny briars;
The golden haunts, burned by the midday sun;
An earthquake brought the wonder palace low;
And now amidst the ruins and ashes, I
Am left alone and palsy-stricken; snakes
And lizards, pains and hatreds dwell now here
In constant loathful brotherhood with me.
An earthquake brought the wonder palace low!

PENELOPE

Wars distant, tempests wild, and foreign lands
Keep thy life-mate for years and years away;

Dangers and scornings threaten thee; and care
With guile and wrath gird thee, Penelope.
About thee, enemies and revellers!
But thou wilt hear, and look, and wait for none
But him; and on thy loom thou weavest always
And then unweavest the thread of thy true love,
Penelope.
Than Europe's goods and Asia's
Even a greater treasure is thy kiss;
Thy loom, much higher than a royal throne;
Thy brow an altar, O Penelope!
Mortals and gods know only one more priceless
Than thine own loom, thy forehead, or thy kiss:
Thy mate, the king thou always longest for,
Penelope. Yet even though strange lands
Keep him away from thee, and distant wars,
And monstrous Scyllas, and the guileful Sirens,
Not even they can blot him from thy soul,
Him, thy thought's whitest light, Penelope!

A NEW ODE BY THE OLD ALCAEUS

To Lesbos' shores, where the year's seasons always
Sprinkle the field with flowers, and where glad
The rosy-footed Graces always play
With the young maidens, once the stream of Hebrus,
Hand-like, brought Orpheus' orphan lyre; and since
That time, our island is a sacred shrine
Of Harmony, and its wind's breath, a song!

The soul Aeolian took up the lyre
Born upon Thracian lands, as foster child;
And on its golden strings the restless beatings
Of Sappho's and Erinna's flaming hearts
Were echoed burningly.
And I, who fight
Always against blind mobs and tyrants deaf,
I, the pride of the chosen few, the stay
Of the great best, returning from exile,
A billow-tossed world-wanderer, did stir
The selfsame lyre with a new quill and breathed
Upon its strings a new heroic breath.
Upon the love-adorned and verdant island,
Like a god's trident, now Alcaeus' quill
Wakens the storm of sounds, and angrily
He strikes with words that are like poisoned arrows
Direct and merciless against his foe,
Whether a Pittacus or Myrsilus.
In vain did tender love reveal before me
On rose-beds Lycus, the young lad, with eyes
And hair coal-black, with rosy garlands bound,
And Sappho of the honeyed smile, the pure,
A muse among the muses, and the mother
Of a strange modesty. Love moved me not!
I raised an altar to the war-god Ares;
And on my walls, I hung war ornaments,
Weapons exulting in the battle's roar.
I sang of the sword bound with ivory,
My brother's spoil from distant Babylon.
I saw my hapless country's ship tossed here
And there, and beaten by the giant waves

Of anarchy; and with my golden Lyre,
Whose voice is mightier than the wild fury
Of a tempestuous sea, I called on War,
The War who revels in men's blood, to come
As a destroyer or deliverer.
And when the war did come in savage din,
Brought upon Lesbos by the might of Athens,
With heart exultant, I saluted him:
"Hail, war of glory!"
Yet, alas and thrice
Alas! Amidst the world of death and ruins,
Though eager warrior and heavy armed,
I felt the solid earth beneath me shake;
My vengefulness, fade into fleeting mist;
My breastplate, press on me like a nightmare;
And my white-crested helmet, like a tombstone!
Confusion was my harbor; and I felt
In me Life's longing win the victory.
And while the nations twain, like maddened bulls
Goad-driven, rushed upon each other's death,
And stern Alecto spread about the flames
Of Tartarus, I saw before mine eyes
—O sight enchanting!—Lesbos' luring shores!
Never before were they so beautiful
With love and verdant! There I gazed on Lycus,
The boy with eyes and hair coal-black that never
Before had touched my heart so powerfully.
And the Muse Sappho of the honeyed smile
Glittered before me, pure and violet crowned;
And her strange modesty bewitched my tongue

With power unwonted until then; and I,
The strong, silently feasted on her beauty!
And while about the maddened Ares raged,
Reaper of men and vanquisher of rocks,
With my soul's eyes, I followed on the trail
Of the Lyre-God, who passed that way, returning
From the Hyperboreans' land. He passed
Aloft, crowned with a golden diadem,
Upon a chariot drawn by snow-white swans,
Towards his Delphic palaces, flower-decked,
With nightingales and April on his train.
Oh, would that I might live to touch them! Would
That I might hold their charms in my embrace,
Those charms so sweet and guileful and divine!
And at the thought—alas, and thrice alas!—
I threw my trusted sword and shield away,
And fled, a shameful coward and a traitor!

FRAGMENTS FROM THE SONG TO THE SUN 1899

IMAGINATION

Imagination, mistress, come!
Come thou leading master, mind!
And you, O tireless workers, come,
Water-Fairies of the Rhythm!
Come, and from Desire's great depths,
And from the Reason's lofty heights,
Bring, oh bring me lasting flowers
Wrought on marble and on gold!
Bring me words of splendid sound!
Build with them the palace high!
And within it raise aloft
The Sun's image all-transcending
Wrought of sunlight gleaming bright!

THE GODS

And the first-born man beheld
The sun rise in the east;
And from within his bosom lo,
A stream of music rose,
An answer sweet to the sun's light,
A music stream of hymns,
Countless words and countless praises
To the fountain of the day!
And—O miracle!—all hymns

And countless words and praises
Spread in waves from end to end!
And taking flesh in time,
They became great gods of light
And signs of harmony!

MY GOD

Wounded with the mighty love
Of my mistress Life,
I wander on, her loyal herald
And her worshipper.
To thy mystic suppers call
Me not, O Galilean,
Prophet of the misty dream,
Denier of things that are!
Crowned with lotus, show me not
Nirvana's senseless bliss!
Yet, do thou, O Sun, shine forth
About, within, above;
Shine upon my love and make
A world of the Earth planet!
Shine life-giving with thy light,
O my Sun and God!

HELEN

*... She gave not me, but made a breathing image
Of the light air of heaven and gave that
To royal Priam's son! And yet he thought
That he had me—a vain imagining!...*

Life Immovable - First Part

Euripides, *Helen*, 33-36.

Helen am I! In the Sun's fountain
Have I taken birth!
I am the Sun-god's golden dream,
And unto him I go!
Not about me, but about
Mine image, which the gods
Had wrought, life's perfect counterfeit,
Recklessly gods and heroes
Plunged into war and war's destruction!
For the Cimmerian
Enchanter carried far away
As his own mate my shade
Thrice-beautiful, that rose to life
From Night's embrace in an
Enchanted land and hour. I am
The bride intangible,
Inviolable, beyond all reach!
Helen am I!

THE LYRE

I know a lyre that is as priceless
As a sacred amulet;
A spirit with a master hand
Made it and cast it here.
No mortal hand of skill or love
Or power rouses it,
Nor makes it answer to the touch
With sound or voice or sigh.

Even the wise and beautiful,
The northwind and the breeze
Cannot awaken the sweet lyre!
Only the Sun-god's beams,
They with one kiss alone can make
Its sun-enamored strings
Sing Siren-like!

GIANTS' SHADOWS

Like moanings of the sea, I hear
Voices ascend from darkness:
Are they the giants' shadows moving?
—Shadow, who art thou? Speak!
—I am the Telamonian!
And see, within me I
Close the whole sun that never sets
Though Hades yawn about;
Weep not for me!
—And thou beside him?
—The heart of Teutons' land
Brought me to life. A maker, I,
Maker sublime of worlds
Olympian, have even here
In Tartarus' dark realm
One longing for my heart, one thirst:
I long and thirst for light!

THE HOLY VIRGIN IN HELL

The chariot moves, drawn by wings
Of Cherub Spirits, on!
In Hell, the Holy Virgin gleams!
"Mercy, O sunlike Lady!"
The damnèd cry and beat their breasts
Amidst the flames that burn,
Fed by the great abyss. Among them,
A sudden proud complaint
Is heard: "A worshipper was I
Of the great Sun; was this
A cause for night to fetter me?
Tell me, O sunlike Lady!
The light of life I sucked, did that
Become the Hell's embrace
And Satan's kiss for me?"

SUNRISE

The white swans gently drag their boats
Of ivory; bright beams
Glimmer as through a veil of agate;
And coral-wrought, the crowns
Shine on fair locks like amber gleaming.
A pearl lake dreamlike lives
With water lilies studded.
Azure-browed Fairies revelling
Quaff wine of honey gold;
And mighty riders steal away
With brides thrice-beautiful.
But thou, an archer mightier,
Risest unmaking all

The multitudes of binding charms
With the one charm of light,
O God of wing-sped chariot!

DOUBLE SONG

The lithesome maiden stood thrice-fair,
Her eyes like gems agleam!
"I pour the crimson wine of love
In empty cups of gold!"
—"Maiden, I am the nestless bird;
Flowery boughs bar not
My way. Bound for bright suns magnetic,
I sail through darkness blind.
Seer am I and worshipper
Of all that is and lives!
I am the harp of thousand strings
Of countless sounds!"
—"Thou blind!
Seest thou not within mine eyes
The magnetism and glory
Of all the suns?"

THE SUN-BORN

On great Olympus, a feast of joy!
The gods divide the earth;
The light-bestower is away;
Forgotten he will be.
And the light-giver came and nodded
To the blue sea; and lo,

The sea was rent with fruitful heave!
And the Sun's island rose
With a thousand beauties crowned;
And makers lived upon the island,
Beings above all men;
And they made statues masterful,
All beautiful like gods
And living as immortals live!

ON THE HEIGHTS OF PARADISE

The little house I built for thee
To dwell therein, enchanter,
Even that—to my care-bent grief—
Becomes a heavy grave.
Yet, little soul of lily whiteness,
Spare me thy sad complaint;
For on the heights of paradise,
I wander longing and
I search. I search and wait for it.
And on the crossroads wide
Of the suns, I shall find a house
Snow-white that even eagles
High-flying never face; a house
That Visions great alone
May touch. Therein I shall enthrone thee!

THE STRANGER

When first the vaulting palm-leaves spread
Their shelter over thee,

The golden Cyclads danced about
With merry shouts and laughter.
But now,—O nakedness of plains
And mountains! Withering
Of green leaves everywhere! Thorns suck
The green blood of the vines!
No April looked on thee again;
And on the desert land,
The wars of elements and beasts
Rage furious. But thee
The snow-white swans bring back no more;
Thou art for ever guest
At the Hyperboreans' feast.

AN ORPHIC HYMN

Far from the footpaths of the thoughtless,
An Orphic priest and bard,
I bring to light again a hymn
Of a thrice-ancient cult.
For until now my thought flowed on,
A river under earth.
Amidst men's tumult my lyre's rhythm,
A sudden wonder rose.
At night I start, at night I climb
The mountain difficult;
I wish alone and first to greet
Light Apollonian
While among mortal men below
Darkness and sleep shall reign.

THE POET

Sun made the lily white,
The glory of the flowery earth;
Sun made the swan, which is
The lily of a life white-winged;
The eagle, whom he lures
Spell-bound to his great heights,
And the gold shimmer of the moon,
The lovers' loving comrade.
And then he dreamed a creature fuller
Of lilies, eagles, swans, and shimmers,
And made the poet. He
Alone beholds thee face to face,
O God; and he alone,
Reaching into thy heart, reveals
To us thy mysteries.

KRISHNA'S WORDS

I am the light within the sun,
The flush within the fire;
And on the page of the sacred book,
I am the mystic word.
The men of mighty deeds call me
Glory; the wise men, wisdom.
Of things existing and of truth,
I am the fountain head!
I am the life of all that is!
Beings and pearls are bound
Together with one thread; and that,

Is I! Maya alone,
The sorceress, behind me follows
Beguiling me. But I
Battle with her to victory!

THE TOWER OF THE SUN

Away beyond the world's far edge,
And where the heavens end,
The tower of the sun shines bright
Dazzling the mortal's mind.
Once mighty princes, sons of kings,
Went on a chase most wonderful,
And stopped at the Sun's tower.
And the Sun came, the dragon star,
The giant merciless!
Woe unto him who lingers there
By the far heavens' end!
And the Sun came; and with his spell,
He turned them into stones,
The princely hunters, sons of kings!
No azure field, no streak of green,
No shadow, and no breath!
Only a death of light and lightning
Glitters about and gleams!
And in the tower, in and out,
As if by masters set,
A world of statues voiceless stand,
The offsprings of great kings.
And from their deep and smothered eyes,
Something like living glance

Struggles to peep through its stone veil!
It seems the stone-bound princes
Wait for a sail, long lingering,
From the world's shores away.
And thou, O princess beautiful,
Camest from far away,
A fair Redeemer! The Sun's tower
Gleamed forth as if the light
Of a new Dawn embraced its walls.
Thou knowest where Life's Fountain
Flows, and thou searchest silently,
With steps that slowly move
Towards the fountain tower-guarded where
Life's water flows. And lo,
Taming the watchful dragon's fangs,
Thou drawest from the fountain
Where the sweet water of Life flows on;
And sprinkling them with it,
Thou wakest up the sons of kings!
And on thy homeward trail,
Thou shinest with transcending gleam,
Like a far greater Sun!

A MOURNING SONG

No! Death cannot have taken thee!
In the sweet hour of love,
The Sun-god lifted thee away,
O child of sunlike beauty!
He took thee to his palaces
To fill thee with his love,

A love that lives in light and is
An endless glittering!
Flowers with light-born fragrances
And fruits as sweet as light,
The Sun will pluck for thee; and he
Will bathe thee in a stream
Flooded with light. And clad
In a white robe of light, my child,
Thou wilt come back to me,
Riding on a star-crowned deer!

PRAYER OF THE FIRST-BORN MEN

Each time the dawn reveals thy face,
Each time the darkness hides thee,
Before the eyes of all the world,
In crimson red thou shinest,
Father and God blood-revelling!
A bath in blood immortalizes
Thine unfathomed beauty!
Blood feeds and veils thee, Father
And God blood-revelling!
To quench thy thirst, we offer thee
Our only children's lives;
And if their blood fills not thy thirst,
We spread for thee a sea
Of all the blood of our own heart!

THOUGHT OF THE LAST-BORN MEN

Where temples sounded with hosannas,
Stones lie dumb in crumbling ruins;
And forgetfulness has swept
Dreams and phantoms once called gods.
Even you are gone, O myths,
Golden makers of the thought,
Gone beyond return!
In the empty Infinite,
Blind laws drive in multitudes
Flaming worlds of endless depths.
And yet neither gold-haired Phoebus,
Who is dead, nor yet the sun,
Who now lives a world-abyss,
None, God or law, upon this earth
Could save us or will ever save
Either from the claws of love
Or from the teeth of death!

MOLOCH

Barbarians defile the land
Where the Greek race was born!
And where the loves flew garlanded,
Night-bats roam to and fro!
And in our night, as a glowworm,
The ancients' memory
Sends forth its greenish counterfeit
Of light! It is a night
That our undying sun cannot
Dispel with its bright beams!
From depths and heights, barbarians

Suck soul and fatherland!
And when with a low moan thrice-deep,
We ask thee, Grecian God,
"Art thou the golden-haired Apollo?"
Grimly thou answerest,
"Moloch, am I!"

ALL THE STARS

When I first looked with wonderment
On thee, O Muse of Light,
The morning star upon thy brow
Shone with bright glittering.
And I said: "More of light I need!"
And as I looked again
On thee, O Muse of Light, the moon
Shone brightly on thy brow.
And "More!" I said and looked again:
And saw the sun agleam!
But still insatiate I am,
And wait to look on thee
When on thy brow, O Muse of Light,
The star-spun sky shall shine!

ARROWS

Thou earnest, Phoebus, lower down
From pure Olympus' heights
Towards the land where idle men
And sluggards worthless dwell;
And on thy lyre thou playedst, Fountain

Of flowing harmonies!
The deaf made answer with their sneers!
The blind, with scornful laughter!
And then to rid the world of filth
And purify the air,
Thou threwest away thine angry lyre;
And turning archer, thou,
With fiery arrows smotest all
The flocks of fools away!

VERSES OF A FAMILIAR TUNE
1900

THE BEGINNING

A wedding guest, I travel far abroad!
The bride, thrice beautiful; the groom, a wizard;
And I ride swiftly to the wedding feast.
The land is far, and I must travel on;
An endless path before me leads away,
But till I reach the end, I check the ardor
Of my swift-footed stallion silver-shod,
And wisely shorten my way's weary length
With sounds that, like sweet longings, wake in me,
Old sounds familiar, low-whispering
Of women's beauties and of home-born shadows.
Then flowers pour their fragrances for me;
And blossoms with no scent have their own speech,
The speech of voiceless eyes that open wide;
Unconsciously I speak my words in rimes
That with uncommon measure echo forth
The flames that burn within the heart, the kisses
That the waves squander on the sandy beach,
And the sweet birds that sing on children's lips!

THE PARALYTIC ON THE RIVER'S BANK

Upon the graceless river bank that spread
Barren and desert, all things drooped in sickness;
And I, with palsy stricken, lay in pains!
Vainly my hands shook feather-like with fever;

Methought my feet were nailed upon the ground;
The river, wide and wild; and far beyond,
As far as eyes could see, the other bank
Revelled in lusty growth and endless mirth
With leafy slopes and forests glistening!
Meadows unreaped and glades untrod were there,
And floods of green and tempests of new blossoms!
About the tree-tops glittered crowns of light;
Shadows thrice-deep hid mysteries divine;
And all descended blindly to the bank
Where the wild river's anger held them back,
Seeking, it seemed, a ford to come across
To the dark bank of wilderness and torture!

And toward me all seemed to stretch their hands,
Sending me shameless kisses as I lay
Parched by the burning wind and worn with fever.
Nearby a sun-dried reed poured forth its sighs;
And farther, a small laurel stirred its leaves:
The double treasure of my wilderness.

I wished to cut a flute from the dry reed
And wished a crown of laurel; but I lay
Nailed down immovable as if the rod
Of an enchantress evil-born had touched me;
And within me, with wings of impotence,
My wounded mind fluttered on hopelessly!
And then thou camest girt with working garb;
With girdle flower-spun, with apron full
Of fruits, didst thou bend over me. The spell
Thou didst dispel and gavest me to eat

And cleansedst me with myrrh; and suddenly,
A soul divine and merciful came down
On the bank merciless; and in thine arms
Lifting me gently, thou didst go forth
Amidst a moaning as of humming bees.
Thou stoodst on the threshold of the peasant hut,
The hut that was earth-built and filled with grass
As if the art of a small bird had wrought it.

Thou didst lay me upon a bed at dusk
That I might rest; and mingled with sweet care
And innocence, thou didst lean by my side
With body ripe and beautiful. Wert thou
A lover, mother, sister, or a woman?
Thou didst lay on my brow thy hand to lull me;
And in thy thoughtful face, I saw the gleam
Of kindly Nausica and good Rebecca.

I slept and woke; even my sorrow's ogress
Had turned into a fairy sweetly sad!
And in my hands I found both, laurel bough
And reed! I drank the fragrant morning breath
Of pines; and taking up the laurel boughs,
I wove with master hand the whole day long
All kinds of laurel crowns for thee; and then
I poured into the unaccustomed air
Of thy small hut a flute's soft-flown complaint.

But from my bed, I lifted up mine eyes
To the window's light and saw again, alas,
The desert river bank, and, far beyond,

The world that squandered diamonds and pearls
And revelled in its joy of green dew-clad.
Again they nodded secretly at me,
Stretching their hands and feigning love!
And even near thee, palsy struck I was,
The paralytic on the river bank!

THE SIMPLE SONG

Thou camest far away from lands beyond!
Thou wert not a gold sunlit cloud at sunset
But mother of a honeyed tenderness
That until then lay hidden in my mind's
Tenderest shrine; the golden seal of a
Young maiden's joy stamped with its touch!
The evening star thou wert not; but thou wert
The sister of a simple love that lay
Hidden till then in my heart's inner depths.

Before me thou didst not unfold the spaces
Of the blue skies; not didst thou lift mine eyes
Towards the rough-hewn peak; nor didst thou open
To me the way for distant palaces;
Nor didst thou lead me by a secret path
Untrod. But lifting with one hand the basket,
Gently thou heldest with the other mine;
And leading me to sit by ferns dew-clad
And deep green grass and snow-white flowers, thou
Badest me stoop and gather; and I stooped
And gathered all my hands could reach: wall-

flowers,
Hyacinths, violets, and daffodils;
And found beside them a May day anew.

Over their petals newly reaped and fresh
That made the basket seem a cruel spring,
I bent and wept for their deaths swift and fair;
And lo, thou didst face them, a Life agleam!

THREE KISSES

A Dream flew down and stood before mine eyes—
Who knows from what unknown deep-hidden nest?
It took the face of my own secret love
And blew me with its hands three airy kisses:

The first air-kiss spread in my breast the din
Of bitter and sweet life in waves of air;
And the world's music sounded manifold,
A tempest's roar and a sweet breath's caress.

The second air-kiss whispered low to me
All whisperings that Silence stoops to sing
Over bare wilderness and tombs and ruins,
Songs that no soul nor even wind can hear.

The third air-kiss would bring to me, it seemed,
Secrets from somewhere heard by none before.
Perhaps, by some bright star, two spirits white
Embraced each other as they passed in thought.

ISMENE

To N.G. Polites, her father.

Where is the little girl and beautiful
Who drew the milk of a full life and precious?
She filled her home with fragrance, and away
She sailed to anchor in another land.

She filled her home with fragrance, and on wings
Swiftly she fled and passed away. Who knows
Why she has left the flesh? Perhaps, she went
Among the mystic joys of things unseen
And things intangible to be herself
Something new, something beyond compare or word.

And yet her house is wrapped in spider webs
And longs for her. To her warm nest, will she
Return? Perhaps, each time you feel, O home,
Within your bosom something sweet and tender
That cannot be explained, it may be she;
Who knows? Then speak to her and say: "Do you,
Too, long for me, O soul without return?"

THOUGHTS OF EARLY DAWN

Who are you that awake me in the morning?
Not the reveille that sweetens with its sounds
The soldier's hardy life. Nor can you be
The chapel bell that slowly rings to prayer.

Life Immovable - First Part

* * * * *

Your steps fall heavy on the road. You bring
Thought, light, and sound, my sacred Trinity.
What if you rouse the slave who goes to work?
What if you call the prodigal to sleep?

* * * * *

Not many were the flowers; and few, the lilies;
And I did long to reap the lily-treasure.
I eyed the lilies all, and walked into
The garden rich to clasp them in mine arms.

* * * * *

And in the garden, all the roses smiled;
Under their veils, the violets bowed down.
I passed them by. The pansies looked erect
And scentless, wrapped in thought: by them, I stopped.
Sweet child, upon thy tomb, a rosebud blossomed;
The hand would reach at it, but it cannot.
And on its path the wind would blow on it;
But ere he light, it dies into a kiss.

* * * * *

Like church lights shine the blossoms in the light;
And butterflies are drunk with airy fragrance;

Yet neither for fragrance nor for light, I come
Into the quiet garden as before.

* * * * *

I come to see the children beautiful,
Running and playing, full of beaming smiles,
Children that make of grassy beds a heaven
And rise like miracles among the flowers.

* * * * *

The brows of righteous men pass slow before me,
Clouds calm and wide, full of refreshing rain;
And from the lightless depths of hell, methinks
I hear breast-beatings and dark blasphemies.
And suddenly, I mingle speech with rime,
The rime that above human things and woes,
Like the Platonic Diotima, rises
A prophetess upon a path sublime
Towards worlds of thought and earth-transcending
loves.

* * * * *

Whatever be thy substance, O bright gleam,
Iron or stone, silver or wind, air-cloud
Or dream, my longing is the same for thee!
Within me thought and hands and art and science
Struggle to build together the same temple.
Maternal Rhea treasures in her breast

All marbles: purple, green, and white. I searched
And found them in your care, Taygetus
Snake-like, and Cyclads fair, and Attica.
And now the columns stand a forest speechless
And motionless; and among them, the rhythms
And thoughts move in slow measures constantly.
And in their depths, light-written images
Show Love that leads and Soul that follows him.

* * * * *

The axe and hammer of the priest black-robed
Struck down the holy idols of the temples;
And yet the soul of the ruins perished not!
It climbed the heaven's spaces as a star
Until new sculptured lilies came to life
In master minds, the gardens of the wise.
Thus axe and hammer of the priest black-robed
Broke not the holy idols of the temples!

* * * * *

Sweet child, upon thy tomb a rosebud blossomed;
Is it thy joy or grief? Thy heart or thou?
If mind, remember me! If mouth, speak forth!
"I am the movement of the motionless,
The lightning flushing from the source of nothing!"

* * * * *

Thy cup is foaming with its black strong wine;
Bring to our fountain thy white-foaming cup,
And brighten into red thy black strong wine
With the fresh water of our fountain here.

* * * * *

I have a thought of dew; a heart of flame!
The wine vat boils; the spring flows fresh and cool;
And I did mingle in my chiseled cup
The black strong wine with the sweet water dew.
A hundred years! A hundred years are gone
Of Grecian mornings and of Grecian sunsets!
Make them a coffin wide, O carpenter,
And bury them, the hapless dead, in silence!

* * * * *

A hundred dragons watch a queen black-robed,
A widowed orphan queen in a lone castle;
And they dig up the scattered fragments of
An ancient and exhaustless treasure, once
Her own, and bring them as their gifts to her!
"I need no fragments! May the hour be cursed
And you, dragons, who hold me prisoner!
I dream of her, the living perfect land
Where I was queen! While here, I am a slave!"

* * * * *

Loud-crying birds that fly toward the heights,
White swans, and swans that cut so tenderly
The silent waters of the lake in thoughts
Of silent sorrow, tameless birds and weary!
O swans that dream the conquest of the sun,
And swans that wait the coming of deep sleep!
Within me lies a far and secret kingdom
Where I can see lake-swans and winds like you!

* * * * *

My banished life has found a home near thee;
And by thy grace, I am thy priest, O Phoebus!
And taking from thy bright divinity,
I made the sun-born maiden to thy glory!
I lifted to thine image my loud praises,
And lo, bells hoarse and tuneless answered them.
Yet what of it? Thine endless praise I am,
And paeans follow on my dithyrambs!

TO A MAIDEN WHO DIED

O little life, quenched by the blow of death
Amidst the tender dreams of rosy dawn,
I cannot lift thee into deathlessness
Upon the chiseled glitter of the marble!
I am a humble bard; and thou, a music
Silenced, whose strains my memory cannot
Recall. Yet with a deeper bond my soul
Thou bindest, O breath unpainted and unsung.

Like a far dawn, thou smiledst in my mind,
A dawn most sweet and shy and fleeting. Then
One day, over my child's pure head thou bentest
With face abloom with smiles and fond caresses.
And something amber-like remained in me
From thee, though thou didst pass; and in the evening
Which in me rises slowly, the dream fairy
Of the azure tales looks with thy face on me.

TO THE SINNER

Sinner, thy mother gave thee not the milk
That makes the cheek a rose, the man a castle!
Each nursing was a sin; each drop, a sickness!
Within thee, ancient lives revive thrice-wretched.

Vices of ancestors unknown and instincts
Of beastly fathers, ever travelling,
Before they rose to light, thus to become
Like smiles and fields of azure blue, came down
To dwell in thee, a people of tormentors!

And one day, sinner, thine own mother gave
To thee the wonder-working holy image
To carry it to the sacred festival
Of the illumined church with open gates
Calling upon its throngs of worshippers.

And on thy way, the luring harlot watched
And stripped thee of thy mind; and as thy hands

Struggled to clasp her, down the image fell,
The sacred image, in the ditch's filth!

And forthwith even there, the plague began
To visit thee! And crumbling down, thou didst
Begin to groan and tremble nearer death
Than the dead corpse on which the ravens feed!
And Satan crouching upon thee rejoices!

And seeing it, thou strugglest painfully,
Stretchest thy hands towards the ditch's filth,
And darest a prayer to the saint defiled,
Though still enflamed by thirst for the vile kiss!

A TALK WITH THE FLOWERS

Upon my passing, slow or swift, by you
I lingered not, nor stooped to pluck you, flowers!
I saw you as a vision skyward roaming,
And I adored you just as thought and sky!
My hand reached not to touch you sinfully,
My flowers! For what is most beautiful
Is also most remote. You were for me
The music that the wind brings on its wings
In perfect strains directly to the heart.
I wished your dazzling could remain as that
Of castles barred and inaccessible.
From far thy fragrance came to me, O jasmine;
And thy gleam, lily, like the eyes' light-kisses!

But since my darling child lay down to sleep
The bitter sleep that knows no wakening,
I am the cruel reaper always bending
Above you, gathering you one by one,
And ever binding you in royal garlands,
And ever weaving you into rich robes
For him! I wish to play new plays with him,
And spread you over him as mine embrace!
I wish to raise him as a flower garden
Breathing into his grave the flower soul
Of an immortal April. Oh, I wish ...
Weak though I am, would all earth's verdancy
Were a long dream and kiss for my beloved!
Would that whatever is beyond man's touch,
Air-born, transcending earth, or fleeting, all
That has a sunbeam as its heart, a breeze as body,
Fair vision, thought, or heaven—would that I
Could close them into forms and scatter them
Upon his flower-clad grave with you, sweet flowers!

In my paternal love, pure white, the flames
Of passion burn; and then, the yellow languor
Of a sick man! Thus did I love him, flowers!
His father though they called me, I was his lover!

O flowers, did you know it? Was your life,
So pure and little, ever touched by such
A woe? Does not a quenchless longing stir you
As you grow on the selfsame flower bough?

The body of my child, sent up from depths
Unfathomed of a secret Fate unhoped,
Was an epiphany of the fair bride,
The bride undreamable, intangible
Of a god's dream! Was he of mine own blood?
I never thought whether he was to live,
Grow, or advance in thought and deed; I was
Drunk with his luring wine, his eyes, his face,
His gait! The breath of blest Makaria
Had blown on him! The stranger's song revolved
Before my mind: "Thou little line so fine,
Written with roses, line that wert his mouth,

How dost thou give birth to that mighty trembling?"

How often when he turned away his lips
So beautiful in careless weariness
From mine embrace, I felt the torturings
Of a disease and drank the bitter draughts
Of jealousy! How often, when he lay
Reclining on mine arms and breathing gently,
I thought I held the graspless image of
Beauty light-born, and said: "What is there more
For me to hope?" O flowers, did you know it?
Can you, too, mingle your little hidden hearts
Fed with sweet honey, the pure frankincense
Of a thrice-blue and earth-transcending worship,
With love's uneasy little tremblings?

Of jealousy! How often, when he lay
Reclining on mine arms and breathing gently,
I thought I held the graspless image of
Beauty light-born, and said: "What is there more
For me to hope?" O flowers, did you know it?
Can you, too, mingle your little hidden hearts
Fed with sweet honey, the pure frankincense
Of a thrice-blue and earth-transcending worship,
With love's uneasy little tremblings?

Oh,
The bitterest and saddest blows, the blows
That know no healing on this earth of ours,
Come from our dearest! Thus he fled and left me
A bitterness beyond all sorrow's pangs,
O little flowers, flowers of dark death!

TO MY WIFE

Here bloomed our home; the young plant verdant blossomed
In the cool shade of the fresh green grape-vine;
And here the mystic moon, entwined in green,
Descended like a first-seen ghost on us.

Here the two fountains of desire refreshed
Our years: the one, before our eyes; the others,
In dreams. The fair Muse silenced here care's crickets
And stirred the sacred frenzy of the lyre.

Here we enjoyed our first-born's flutterings;
And here the little gleaming face and round,
Our second fruit, maddened us with pure joy!
As the unhoped return of a longed friend,
Here we received one day into our bosom
The transitory child beyond compare,
The third one, who transformed the worldly air
About us into flowing wine for gods,
An offering unto the gleaming light
Of high Olympus, dwelling of the blessed!

Here was thy youth, even when care oppressed thee,
A fair Venetian painting, the blithe work
Of a light-beaming Titian, that revealed
Pure shining joy in thy lithe body's form.

Here bloomed our home; the young plant verdant blossomed,
Hidden in the cool shade of the green vine.
Now, nothing remains. Only the mystic moon
Weeps in a palace voiceless, wide, and gloomy!

The life that died here wished for April as
Grave-digger, and a flower-bed as grave.
Oh, who had cursed it? Nothing but a tomb
Was found for it! A tomb unfit and graceless!

THE ANSWER

Take me and hear me, Hamadryads fair,
And Aegipans, Wood-Nymphs, and shepherd gods!
The bridal beds are set! The forest glades,
In flurry! The Flower Festival has come!
The bacchic revelry bursts forth in glow
And frenzy! Where is nature and where is
Its end? I know not whether I am myself;
Great Pan, it seems, dwells in my bosom here.

O wonder! I do live the holy life
And wild of purest nature's elements!
O God of the golden crown, the three fair Graces
And the Nine Sisters of the Song gave me
The gift of tranquil visions beautiful!
I filled me with the foam-begotten beauty
Of all! I hear the nightingales' sweet song
In answer to the song of Sophocles!
The woes of Aeschylus resound prophetic,
Ocean-born! Face to face with me, as swift
As glance, green-clad Atlantides rise forth
From the abyss and sink in it again.

Phoenicians battling with the sea brought me
From far away; I am the reveller
World-wandering! Arts, talks, and images
Are bristling in the air! Take me, O Nymphs
Into your bosom! Satyrs, hear my words!

Yet Satyrs, Centaurs, Hamadryad Nymphs,
And golden-spoken Hellades at once
Made answer to my pleading with one voice
From cities, mountains, forests, cliffs, and plains:

"Gods' wine is not for thee, O reveller!"

And the lithe Tanagraean maiden spoke
With awe-inspiring prophetess Cassandra,
Ivy-crowned Maenads, Gods Olympian,
And the song-nourished Hellades; they spoke
From the far cave of fair Calypso to
The wisdom-haunted Alexandria:

"Silence! Pale monk and idle chatterer!
Silence! Turn back to thy lone cloister cell."

And the Pindaric heroes laugh in scorn
With the white goddesses of marble wrought
By Scopas' hand; laugh, and their laughter-peals
Are echoed loud and deep from far away!

THOUGHT

More than the godlike gleams of sculptured stone,
More than the golden rhythms the poet weaves,
Who knows if a good act unknown, some wound's
Balsam, shines not with brighter lasting beams?

Who knows if for some god's unfailing ear,
The dogged sin and filthy vice are not

A thrice-wise and tempestuous harmony
Of melodies sung by Virtue's lips serene?

Bright shine the temples of Fair Art; bright shine
The rainbows heavenly of Thought; and bright,
The chariots of warriors triumphant!
Yet in the temple of the Universe,
Can they be costlier than the mute Thought
And Glory of the flower, at whose birth
The dawn rejoices and whose early death
The saddened evening silently laments?

The thoughtful sage high-rising smites the gates
Of the Infinite and questions every Sphinx;
Yet who knows if the soldier with no will,
Obeying blindly, is not nearer Truth?

O struggle vast! Who knows what power measures
The measureless and creates the great?
Is it the matchless thought of the endowed,
Or the dim soul of multitudes that bursts,
Thoughtless of reason, into life? Who knows?

The holy man lifts up his hand to bless
With readiness; yet who needs more such blessing?
Is it the free-born bird that makes its nest
Wherever its strong wings would waft it, or
The flowery plant bound by a bit of earth?

Which is the light of Truth? Is it the Law
That is all eyes or is it some blind love?

What leads us there? The hidden path where bent
And trembling we seek our way, or the wide road
That makes us fly with wingèd confidence?

O Thought, thou dream-crowned maiden, ever wrestling
With a blood-filled, swift woman masculine,
Whose bosom, thine or hers, is doomed to yield
The destined milk to nourish and to heal
Our sickened life with health Olympian?

O Thought, thou angel, ever wrestling on
With a strong giant flinging his hundred hands
About thy neck to strangle thee, wilt thou
Battle with sword or lily? Oh, the world
Will crumble ere thy struggle finds an end!

THE SINNER

O hapless one, when thou wert born, there came
The Fate thrice-blessed and clasped thee in her arms
To bless thee with a hero's mighty deeds
And wrap thee in the purple of a king,
The Fate whose blessings teem with light and might.

Yet there, the other Fate, the bitch of ruin
Unspoken and of voiceless death, kept watch;
And she led thee away from the blue shore

With lilies sown, to the salt marsh of terror
And the sheer precipice of fearful trembling!

Nor could thy baby hands grasp more than this,
A cheerless tatter from the sacred veil
Of thy good mother Fate, the veil embroidered
With the star-spangled sky by master hand!

O hapless One, while virgin joy bathes thee
Abundant and thy tears are yet a baby's,
Something within thee groans, the muffled madness
Of fettered murderers, the madness of
Lone cells. And while thou showest the calm life
Of tame things and of love in thy still nook,
Thou breedest fettered wraths and bridled hatreds.
Should they burst forth, ruin and wilderness
Would reign.

O hapless One, the greenest spots
Even of thy existence are but full
Of pitfalls opened wide and yawning void!
No dawning was thy lot; even those boughs
Young of thine early years were parched with drought!
Whatever white thou touchedst was defiled!
And thine old age, if thou couldst bare thy youth,
Would shriek with fear and fly from thy youth's face!

A sneering power or a grace divine
Mercilessly nailed down thy hands and will,
O cowardly, decrepit, idle man,
Infirm and hapless, starless night enclosed
In a weak child! Death will not come to thee
As to the toiling laborer who toils
The whole day long, and towards evening, sleep,
Even before he lies, in bed to rest,
Creeps sweetly upon him and seals his eyes.

Thy death shall be laden with graspless horror
Such as one feels who sinned in secrecy
And dreads each hour detection of his sin,
Trial, death sentence, and the hangman's rope.

O hapless One, would that in thy death struggle
Her bosom might still shine before thine eyes,
The good Fate's breast, who blessed thy birth with goodness,
The Fate whose blessings teem with light and might!
Would that thou couldst show her the humble shred
Torn from the star-wrought sacred veil of hers
And tell her: "See, in the deep darkness smiles
Something, a dawn on which I still hold fast!"

O hapless One! Would that the mighty heroes
And royal purples and the blessings full
Of light and might and all thou knewest not

In thy dark empty life could shine upon
Thy passing as the lights of distant stars!

THE END

A wedding guest, I travel far abroad!
The bride, thrice-beautiful; the groom, a wizard;
And I ride swiftly to the wedding feast.
The land is far, and I must travel on;
An endless path before me leads away.

And the far land a vision was! The steed,
A smoke! The wedding, angels' shadows fleet!
While I,—O cruel wakening!—lie down
For ever palsy-stricken and bed-ridden!

And only you, old tunes familiar,
I hold. I hold you as a dying darling child,
Languid and glowing with the fever's heat,
Holds on to his dear plaything, with white wings
New-grown for his long journey, even I,
The child unskilled, dream-roaming, stript of will!

Old tunes familiar, waft me upon
Your shining wings for healing or for death
To the cool shadow of the pure-white home
And lay me gently on a loving bosom.

THE PALM TREE

TO DOSINES, WHO HEARD IT FIRST.

Once in a garden about a palm tree's shade, some blue flowers, here very dark and there very light, talked with each other. A poet who now is dead, passed by; and he put their talk into these rhythms:

O Palm Tree, someone's hand has cast us here;
Was it the hand led by a cursed Fate,
Or moved by mind of good intent? Who knows?
What impulse seized us from the cave of sleep
Below to bring us to the surface here?
Is it a savior's or destroyer's power
That sets us motionless beneath thy shade?
And is thy shade the shade of life or death?

* * * * *

The glare of the hot sun drowned everything;
Gluttonous locusts groped for food about;
And then, a rain. The flowers, that had drooped
To sleep, awake to drink the drops of dew.
And then, the clear sky's festival begins
More azure than before to spread above thee.

Only thy trembling crest drops here and there
Some large and shining rain-pearls on the earth.

* * * * *

The garden glitters with a new-born life;
And each bird dreams it is a nightingale;
Only from thy lone heights like bullets fall
Thy pearl-clear drops, and oh, the pain thereof!
The dew drops make a crown for everything;
The gurgling waters are a balm to all;
Why should this god-sent goodness of all things
Be blow for us and suffering and flame?

* * * * *

How cruelly thy bullets fall and smite!
No ear above and not an eye before us!
Beneath thy shade we live; thy trunk is world
To us; thy crown, a star-spun sky, our sky!
If thou art a god merciless, reveal
Thyself! If not, but nod and give us calm!
Either cease slaying us one by one, or pour
On us at once a flood to drown us all!

Our pain is as reward and treasure found!
The golden seal of harmony has stamped us,
And while Death touches us, we glory, victors!
We tremble; hail O rhythm's thrice-sacred tremor!
A worm may live sunless beneath the earth
That a new butterfly of silken wings
May live an hour of perfect life and die.
The wound's gash turns into a living fountain!

*****

Things gray, things crystal, myriad hues of green,
Gushings of fountains clear, and caterpillars,
Earth's things immovable, air-sailing ships,
And little worms, and bees, and butterflies,
Sweet flower-grails and censers, fondling grass,
The moss-down's countless kisses, echoes from
Below, and mandolins ethereal,
Leaves quivering and lilies languor-bringing!

*****

The turtle-doves know not what you know, blossoms,
The chosen things of beautiful loves, you!
Kisses and starts and wooings of the boughs!
The birth of each of you is a world's dawn!
You know, O little tearful short-lived things,
You know pleasure's and joy's eternities!
We, the gold garlands wreathed about thy root,
Are like celestial and thoughtful eyes!

*****

Blithe flowers, boughs that hang with blossoms full,
From dandelions to the chamaemele,
You may be like the glowing coals or gems,
Or like a maiden's rosy cheeks and lips.
Though you, like hands, may open full or empty,

Life Immovable - First Part

And though you be dawn's smiles or evening's candles,
Or the fair palaces of Fairy Dew,
The gazing eyes are we! We are the eyes!

* * * * *

Though small we are, a great world hides in us;
And in us clouds of care and dales of grief
You may descry; the sky's tranquility;
The heaving of the sea about the ships
At evenings; tears that roll not down the cheeks;
And something else inexplicable. Oh,
What prison's kin are we? Who would believe it?
One, damnèd, and godlike, dwells in us; and she is Thought!

* * * * *

Frolick, and form, and wanton playfulness,
And some unspoken radiant vanity,
And some enrapturing bewitching charm,
And perfect virgin beauty are your own!
Fading like gods' pale images, you seem!
Even the bird sometimes bows to your grace!
And Nereids wind-footed fan your faces,
O roses with a thousand smiles divine!

* * * * *

A god commanded it, the flower-haired April!
"O flowing fragrance, change to brilliancy!"
Thus you are scentless, roses of Bengal;
All others' perfume is bright light in you.
And thou, O lily, king among the flowers,
From what far world hast thou been led astray?
Was it from fragrance's own womb, or from
The whitest star? And we, O Palm? Who knows!

River ethereal of fragrance, stay!
Thou hast not flowed nor watered us at birth.
We said to fragrance: "Cease thy flowing course;
Well not from us; nor be our breath! Sink deep
Into our heart's recesses; close thyself
Regardless of thy perfume in our soul!
Then seek to find our thought and live with it
And flow from it as honey from the bee!"

* * * * *

"Bring forth from the rich treasures of the sun
All colors, flowers, and deck yourselves with them!"
We said unto our little brothers: "Make
Robes of the heaven's rainbow for your raiment!"
And to ourselves we said: "Soul, I
Shall let aside all brilliance! I need not
Sunset or dawn; enough would be something
Of the great sea and of the heaven's smile!"

* * * * *

Life Immovable - First Part

Become a cloud, O great Desire, and speak
With lightnings and with thunders! Rise, a lark,
And sing and soar towards a new starry garden!
Turn all thy flooding music into love,
Mingle with it all children's innocence
And all the beauty that is thine; still thou
Wilt have love's shadow only but not love.
For love shines, burns, illumines quenchlessly!

* * * * *

The garden draws life from a triple soul,
A soul that spreads creeping upon the earth
With roots beneath and wings above. A city,
The caterpillar builds in its great depths;
The bird builds love towards heights ethereal!
About all green things live to be thy slaves
And trimming ornaments, O palm! How high
Skyward thou raisest thy grace-moulded body!

* * * * *

No ivy limits and no offshoot mars
Thy trunk's unchained and chiseled nakedness;
And yet, though naked, with a charm dream-
wrought
Thou coverest the alleys of the garden.
And as an emblem of thy reign, a crown
Of beams pearl-born and silver-born shines bright
As it hangs trembling from thy top, O palm.
Oh what a rhythm governs thy form divine!

*****

So beautiful is not the cypress young
As it waves towards the sky, moved by the breeze!
So beautiful is not the mossy fountain
That sings like bard and nourishes like mother!
So beautiful is not sunrise or sunset!
Another world's day hangs from thy high crest!
So beautiful is not the tranquil lake!
Gods and their hymns god-sung are at thy feet!

*****

Neither an angel's shade in a hermit's cave,
Nor harmony's voice in Night's deep silence,
Nor the great maker's thought just as it dawns
In his wide-fronted heaven, and is still
A maiden dream unyoked before it finds
A dwelling in the form of word or music,
Color or marble! None of these is like
Thine image caught and mirrored in our thought!

Is it transparent and immortal blood
That flows in thee, or sap too weak to wake thee
From thy long spell of blind and voiceless sleep
Into a crystal life's fair revelry?
Is thy head's crown another's counterfeit,
Or thine own locks that smitten by the wind
Become stringed lyres to sing in murmurs sweet
Of the world's symphony and of thy beauty?

* * * * *

Neither thy boughs nor locks they are, but wings
That thou wouldst ply with gentle flutterings!
Wings? They are not, though they become; and ever
A hunger tortures thee, and ever thou
Strugglest to enter a sublimer world!
Right, left, high, far, thou seekest a fair city,
Some sunlit Athens, and standest bent on flying
With swans and cranes towards the azure heavens.

* * * * *

Art thou a relic of a dead age and great,
Or the first dew of a becoming life?
Now some Wood Nymph bound within thee peeps out
Struggling to flow into the light about;
And now thou risest like the column last
Of an old temple that once stood in Hellas.
Evening or morning, end or a beginning,
Something binds thee to skies beyond all sight.

* * * * *

Hosannas from thy boughs and palm leaves flow,
Hosannas from thy royal height, as prayer
To some unknown god's charms, who passes by
Revealing his fair godhead first to thee.
And lo, the hillsides answer thine hosannas!

Oh, what thy visions, what thy secrets are?
Some tremor, from new heavens wafted, makes
The supple flowers and green leaves quiver.

* * * * *

And we? The migrant bird did come to us;
The passing wind did touch us with its wing;
The restless brook did check its rapid course;
The child did cast on us his guileless glance;
The jonquil proud did greet us with a nod;
And the moon did look down to see us here;
And all beheld our surface; none our depths!
Thus the world glided over us and vanished!

* * * * *

Sweet orange blossoms, what asked the
nightingales?
What would the dry cicala know of noontide?
All things that groan from the great depths of
earth,
All songs that mount exultant to the stars,
The eating moth's faint voice, the restless cricket's,
Perfumes and breezes, creatures lone and mated,
All things that fly and creep and bend and stoop,
Something they know of thee and hide it from us.

* * * * *

Life Immovable - First Part

Within our breasts, a soul of storm and pitch
Puts into our minds evil thoughts of thee.
The magpie chatters long to the night bat
Of thee; the locust boasts she is like thee;
The wasp draws ample pleasure in thy shelter;
And the night raven finds delight in thee.
A world of evil and of scorn lies wait
For thee who mountest tranquil to the stars.

O Health blown from the heart of the pure pine!
Where thy feet tread, fruits grow 'midst thorns and clover;
If with the streams thou flowest, the elements
Shine; for pure wine, thou reapest the fair clusters;
And where thou lingerest, a city rises!
Thy breasts flow ever with milk; thy lips with dew!
O mother fruitful, strong, and whole, some ill
Rots us and we are pale like death's faint tapers!

* * * * *

Boughs, tresses, wings; shadows whose grace divine
Frolics and spreads as bough or tress or wing;
Another night, you took another form
In the enchanted pitiless moonlight,
A form that was neither bough, tress, nor wing:
Swords you seemed, ready to descend and smite!
Night's roaming butterfly, be merciful!
Lift us upon thy wings and fly away!

* * * * *

Illness and wakefulness have tortured us,
O palm, and we saw thee bend secretly!
The dragon's heads and dogwoods were awake;
We saw thee leading a strange dance with them
At night; and in our first sleep, we beheld thee
A heavy dream roaming with mulleins and
Chameleons; about thee closed whole gardens
Of thistles, aloes hard, and hosts of briars!

* * * * *

We dreamed and lo, thou wert demanding tribute
Of life, blood-drenched; and in thy being raged
A savage hunger; and some beast flesh-eating
Nestled in thee and gnawed a hole through thee;
And thy winged body turned into a cave;
A vulture perched as crown upon thy head;
And like fire-flames, and sea-waves, and sword-
blades,
From root to top, fierce snakes crept up and coiled!

* * * * *

Who ever thought of it? What Fate has ruled
That from ill-smelling things and worthless stuff
Should rise things of resplendent green? and from
Deforming filth, the thrice-pure miracle
Of May and April? Hence things blue and black
Mingle in us; and in our souls, spread oceans
And narrow paths; and while our minds converse

With things sublime, something thrice-base defiles us!

* * * * *

O Sun, assail and strangle all black dreams,
Our life's dim vapors and ill-working demons!
But nourish all things good and beautiful
Like sunbeams playing and like nightingales!
And thou, O moon, spread over savage Night
A veil translucent of heart-felt sympathy!
Wave everywhere, O Beauty's purple robe!
Let the great world be love and love's sweet lyre!

* * * * *

Day comes! Light scatters a thousand eyes on thee
So that thou mayest greet the woods and mountains,
The nests upon the trees, the palaces
Of cities, and the ships on open seas
Or ports. At nights, mounted on steeds of light
Beautiful Fairies come from high to serve thee;
The poplar lifts its many hands to thee;
And the dark cypresses lull thee to sleep.

With pelicans and eagles thou conversest,
And drop by drop thou drinkest the world's music;
Thou seest things far, things near, and things above;
Things infinite, intangible, and great;

And thou communest with air-sailing ships,
Light-rays, and wings, and the world-mounting ladder;
While we, bent low, and lashed by sorrow's whip,
Listen to the great throbbing of Earth's heart!

* * * * *

We heard it, the great throbbing of Earth's heart,
The new song inconceivable, unheard,
Of consummate and perfect sound!
Through it, some thunder-stricken angel groans;
All April's gardens breathe in fragrant balms;
Some unfulfilled and secret longings weep;
And a fire crackles that will ruin worlds!
Something that passes by, an endless riddle!

* * * * *

Tell thou the sunlit story of the air;
We shall unroll to you the tale of blackness.
Come, let us mingle the two elements,
Thy mighty power with our own winning grace!
In unseen places, small and cold and sunless,
A world of workers and of corsairs dwell;
And there are paths and deeds of theirs, and days,
And what the infinite air-spheres have not!

* * * * *

Life Immovable - First Part

A swarm of bees has told us of their life,
And a new youth and wise shone unto us!
The grass hides unsuspected miracles;
Beside us, the ant opens a deep path;
A lizard, slowly creeping from below,
Brought us here news of countries, nations, arts;
A butterfly on her swift flight to wed
The little flowers broadened our world of thought!

* * * * *

Unwedded, fruitless Palm, fair mystery!
Strange was the hour—who will believe it now?—
The divine world willed to become a thought,
And thought revealed itself unto our mind!
Now, unto darkness and to riddles new,
Our little life is ready to depart!
O Palm, make answer; lo, before thou speakest
Thy word sublime, a hand lays wait to smite!

* * * * *

O Palm, a hand did spread to sow us here;
That hand will spread again to root us out,
And we shall die! The billow and the wind
And the still waters will sweep us away
Mercilessly! The flowery spring will not
Lament us! The wide world will never know
We perished! And beneath thy shadow's charms,
Another fragrant race will rise to life.

* * * *

Nor will there be a monument for us
That might retain the phantom of our passing!
Only about thee will a robe of light
Adorn thee with a new and deathless gleam:
And it shall be our thought, and word, and rime!
And in the eyes of an astonished world,
Thou wilt appear like a gold-green new star;
Yet neither thou nor others will know of us!